This Book Belongs to

_____

_____

_____

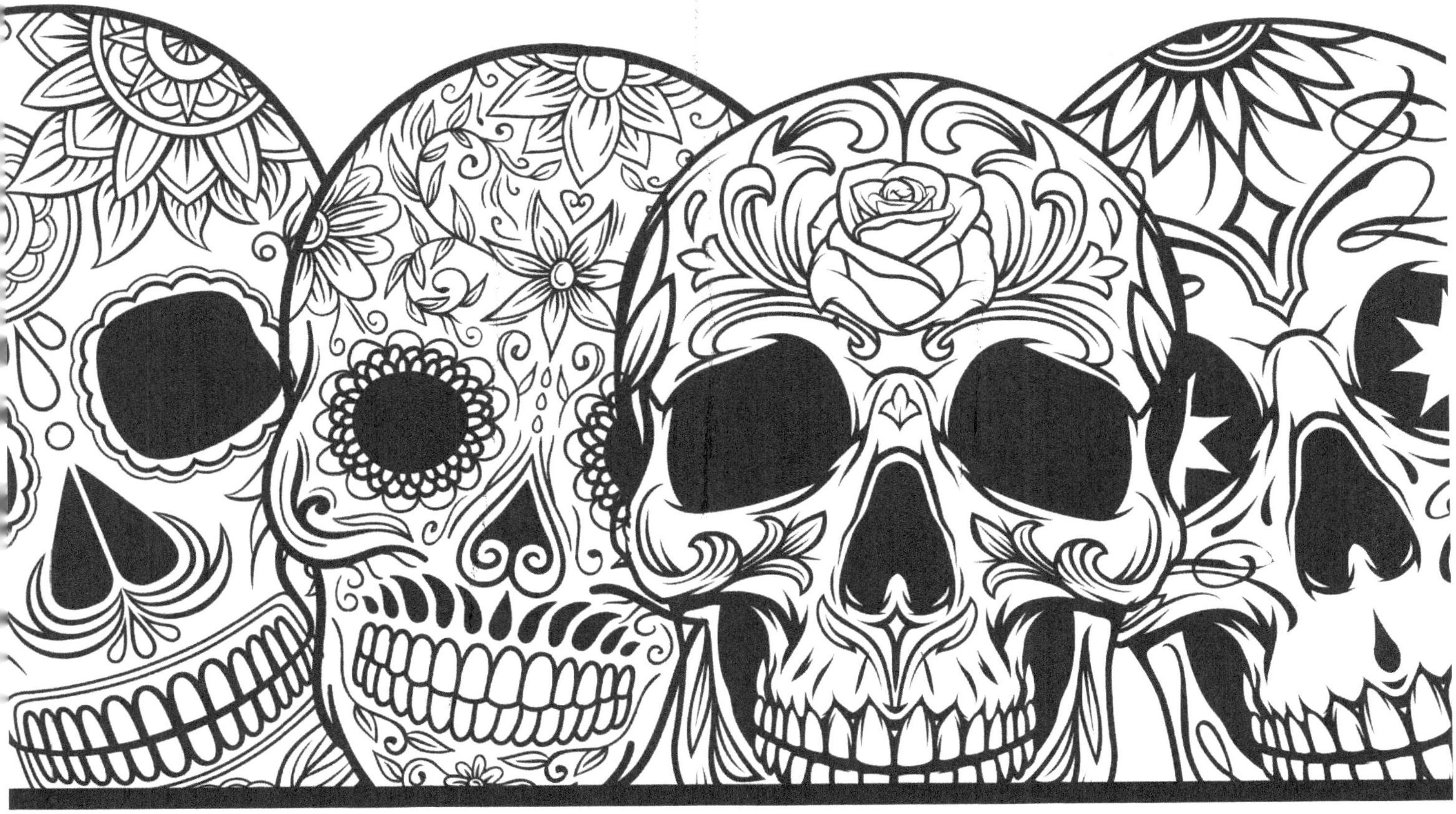

THE PAGES ON THE LEFT ARE BLACK-BACKED TO AVOID COLOR BLEEDING TO THE NEXT PAGE.

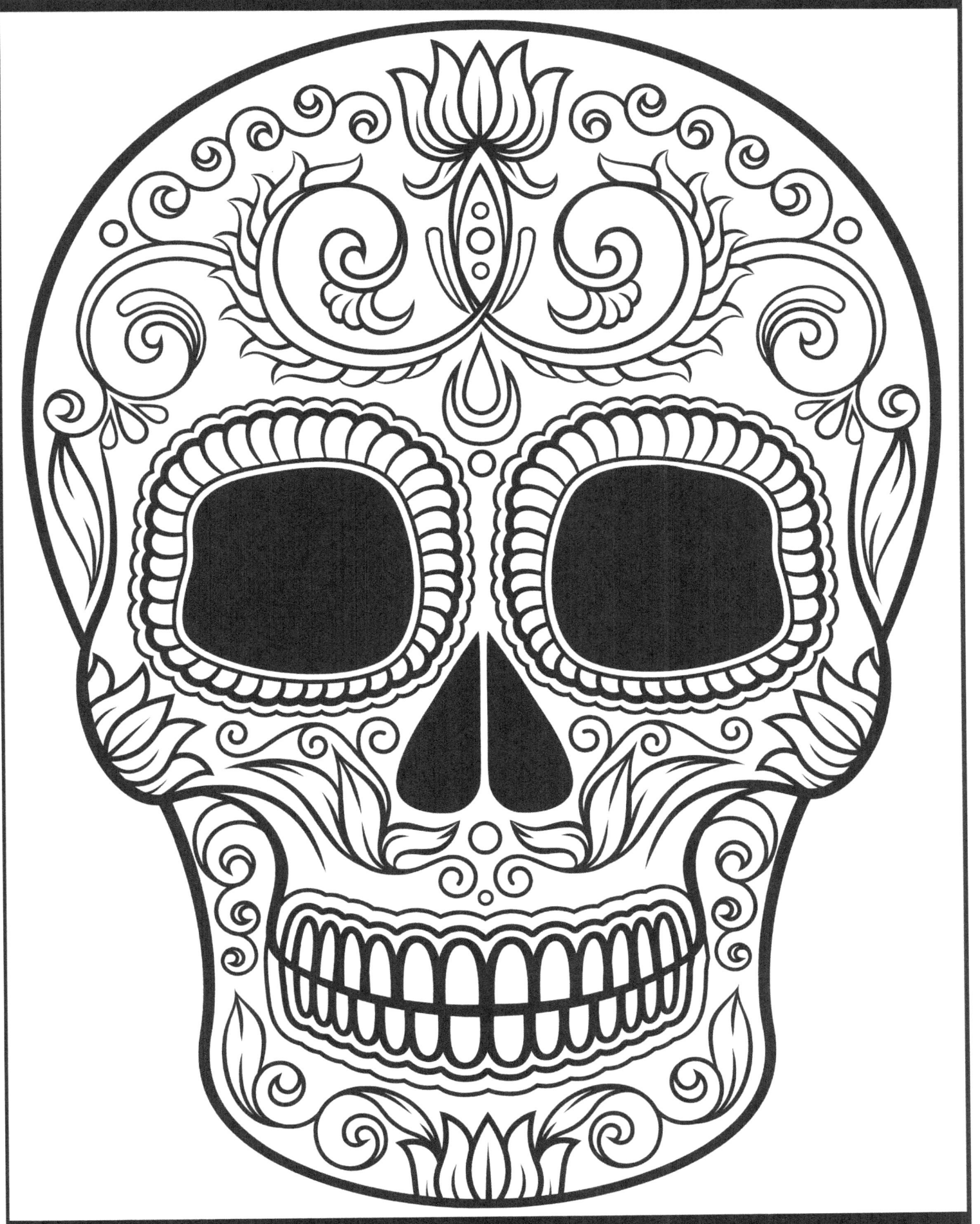

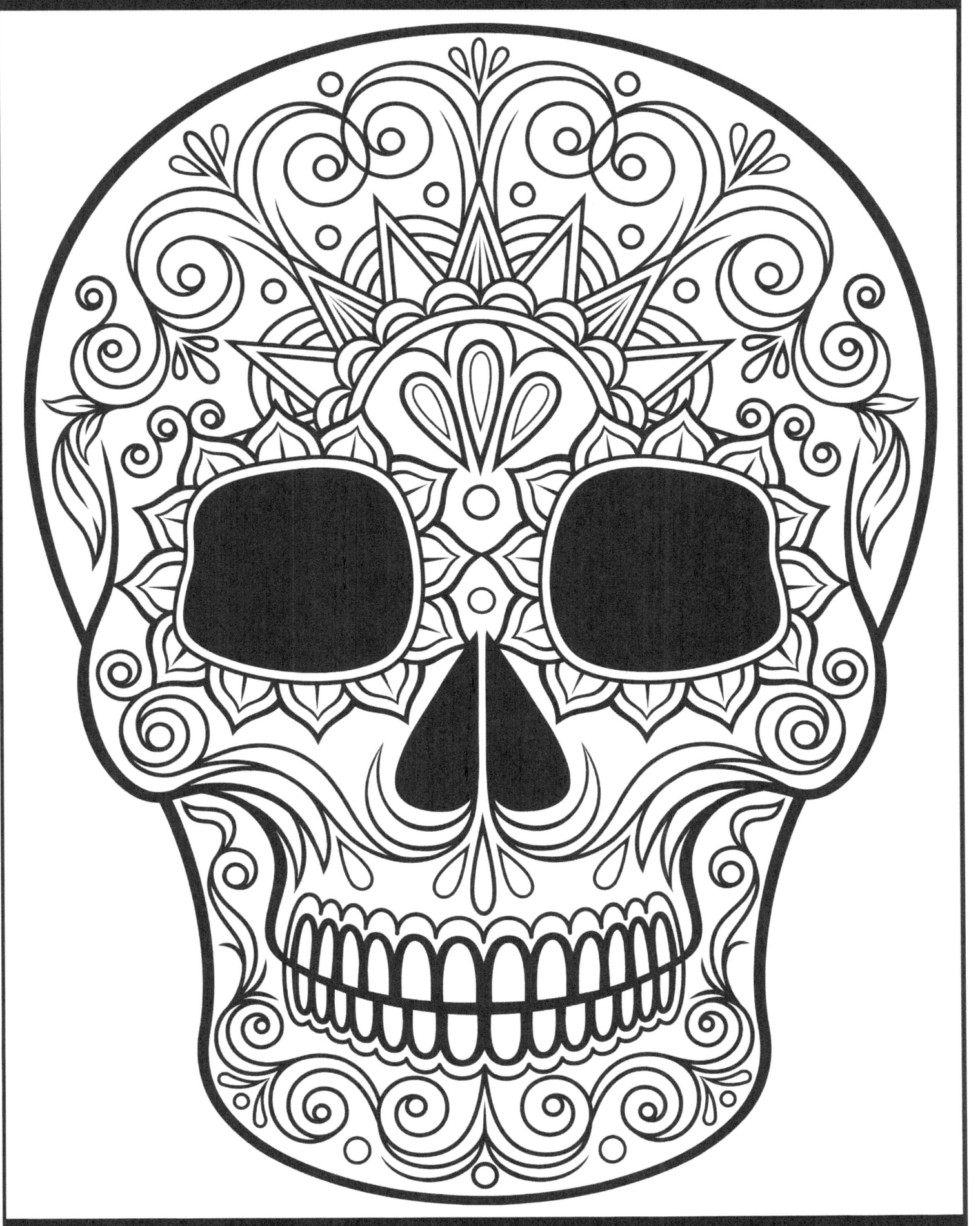

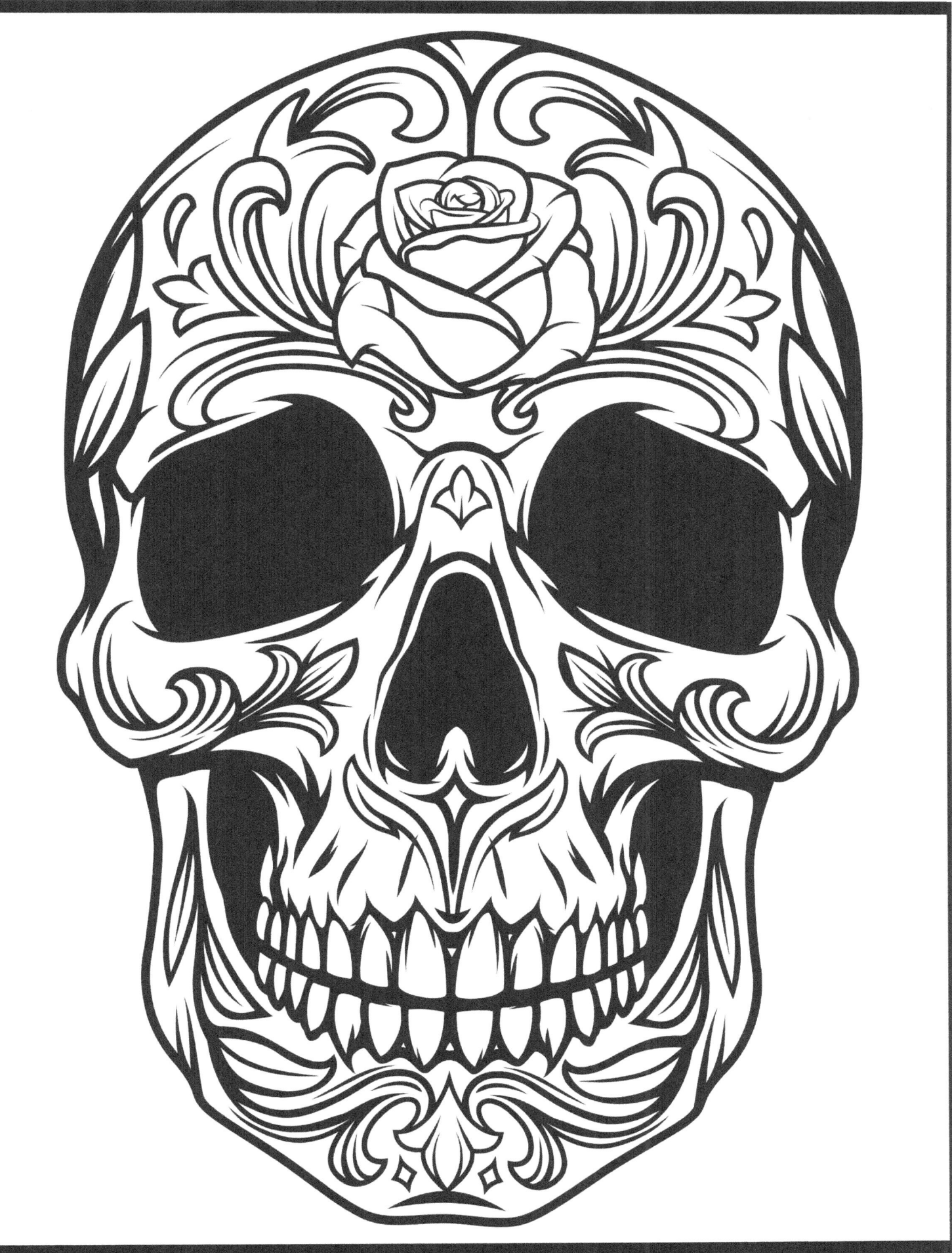

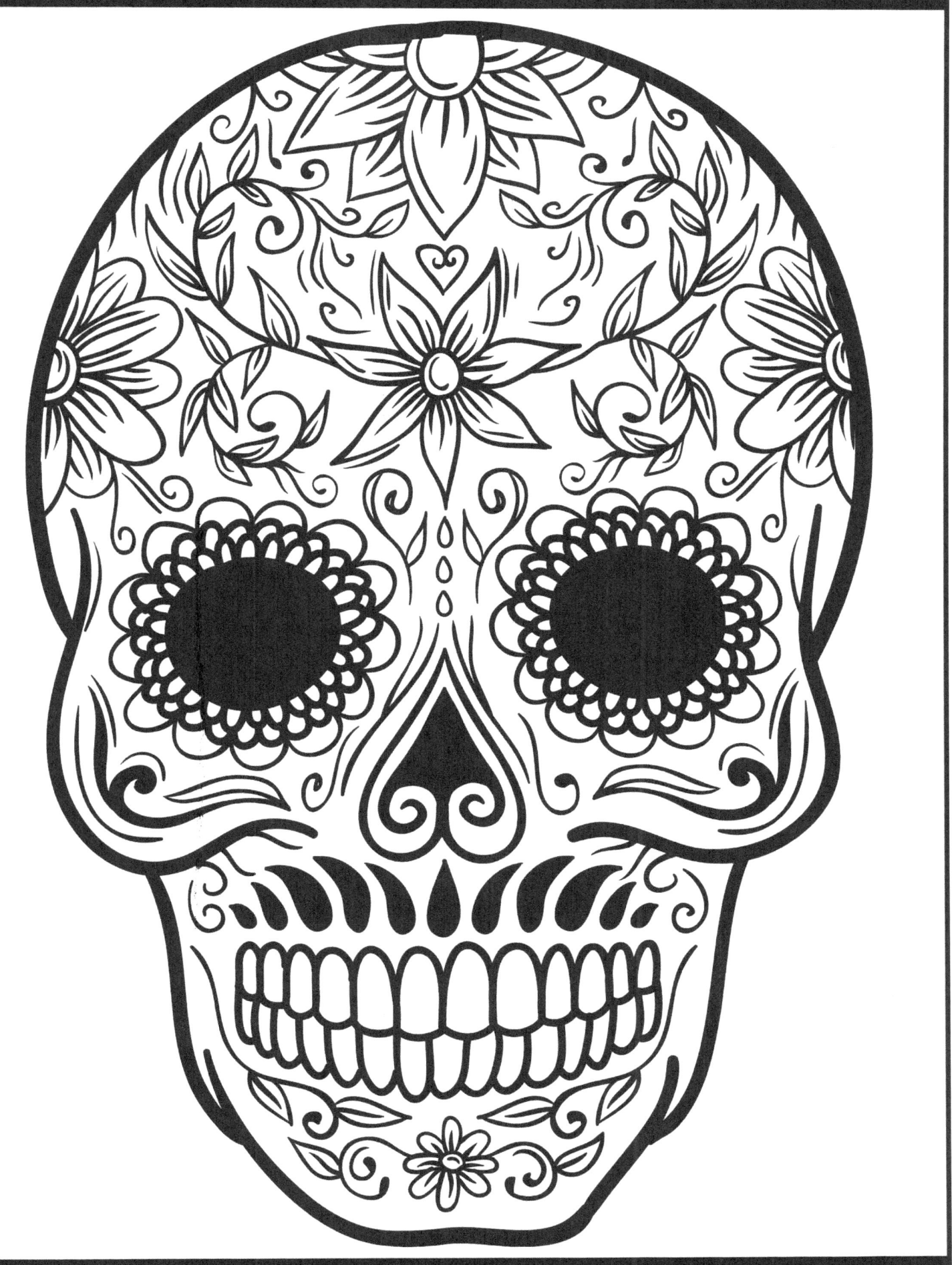

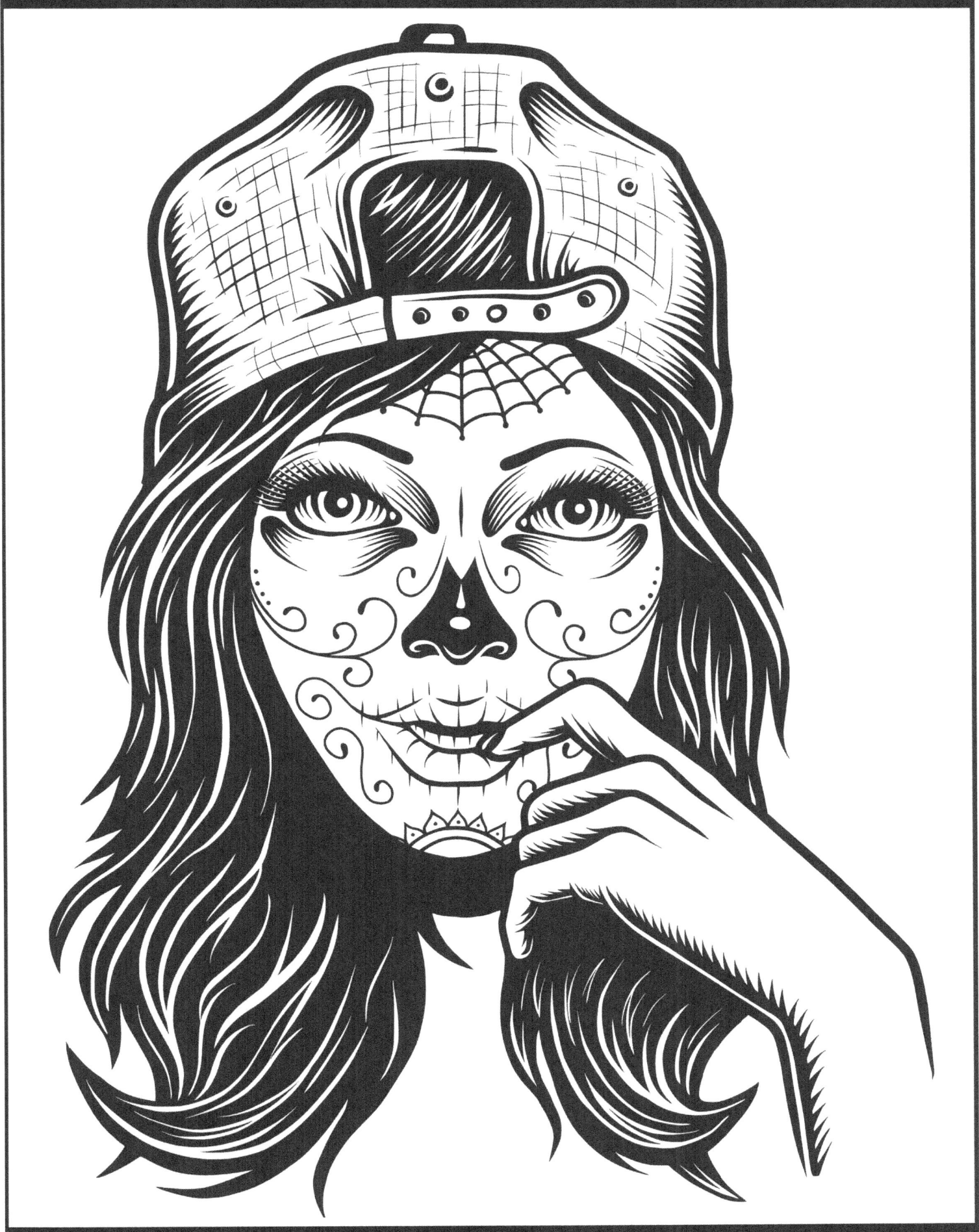

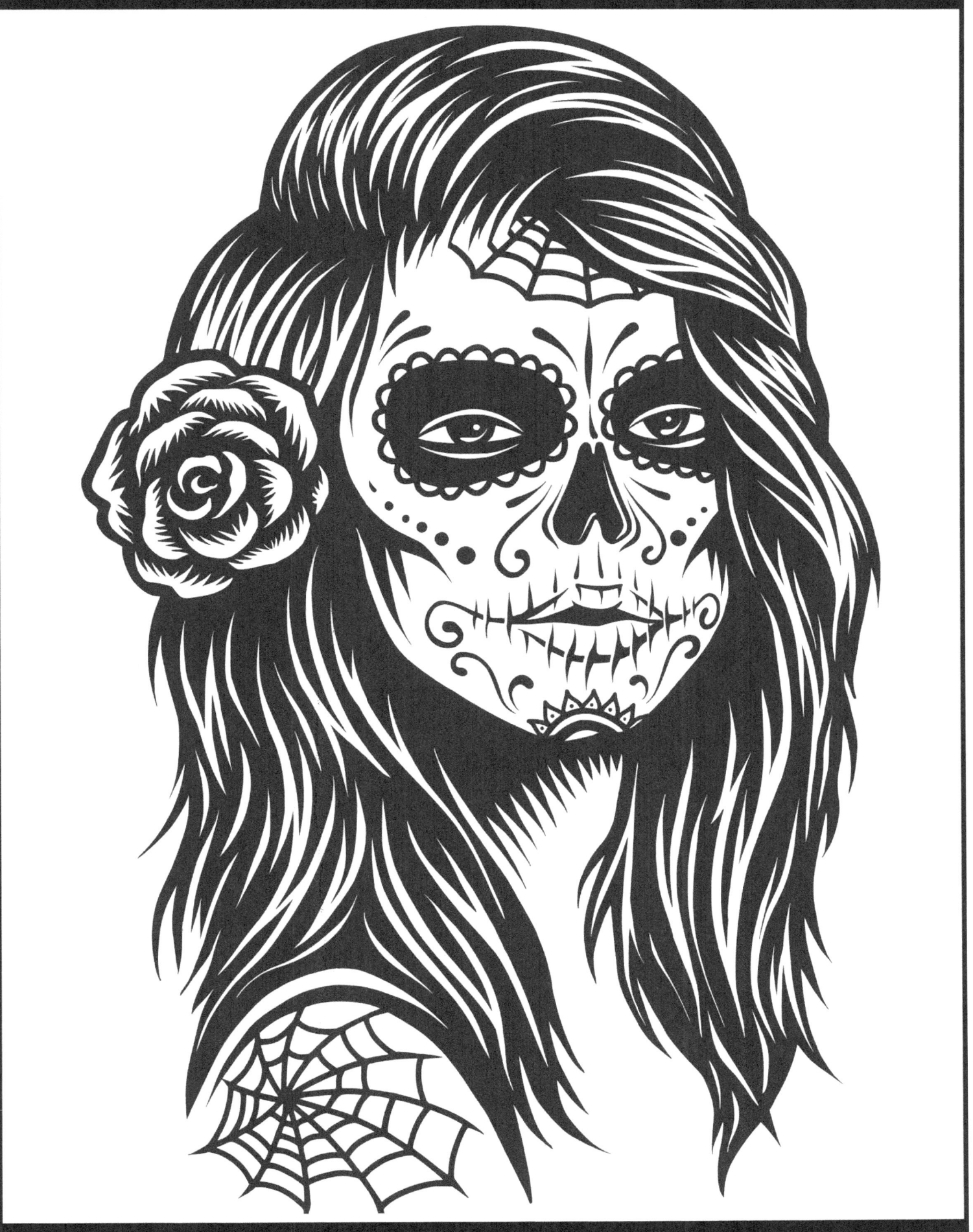

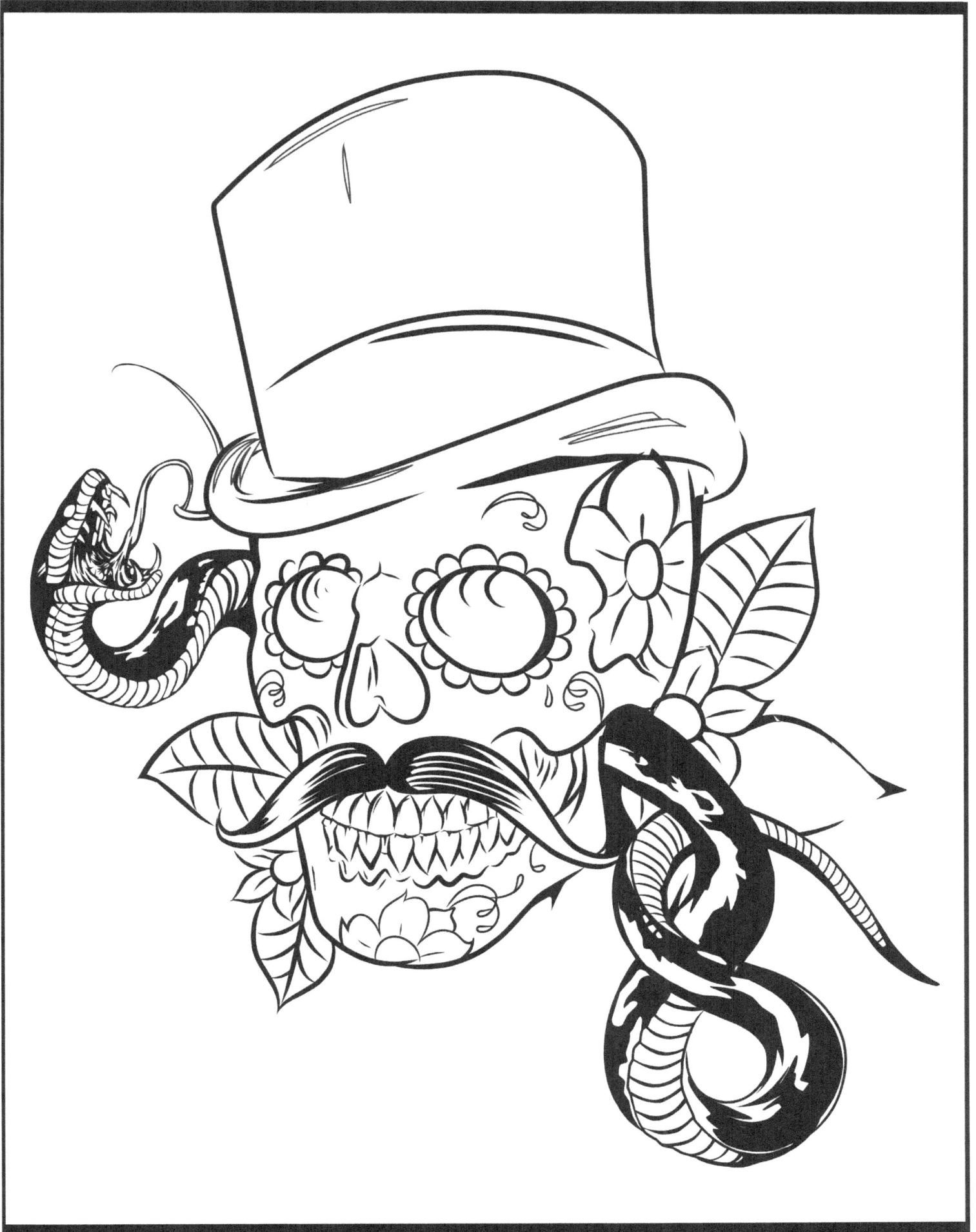

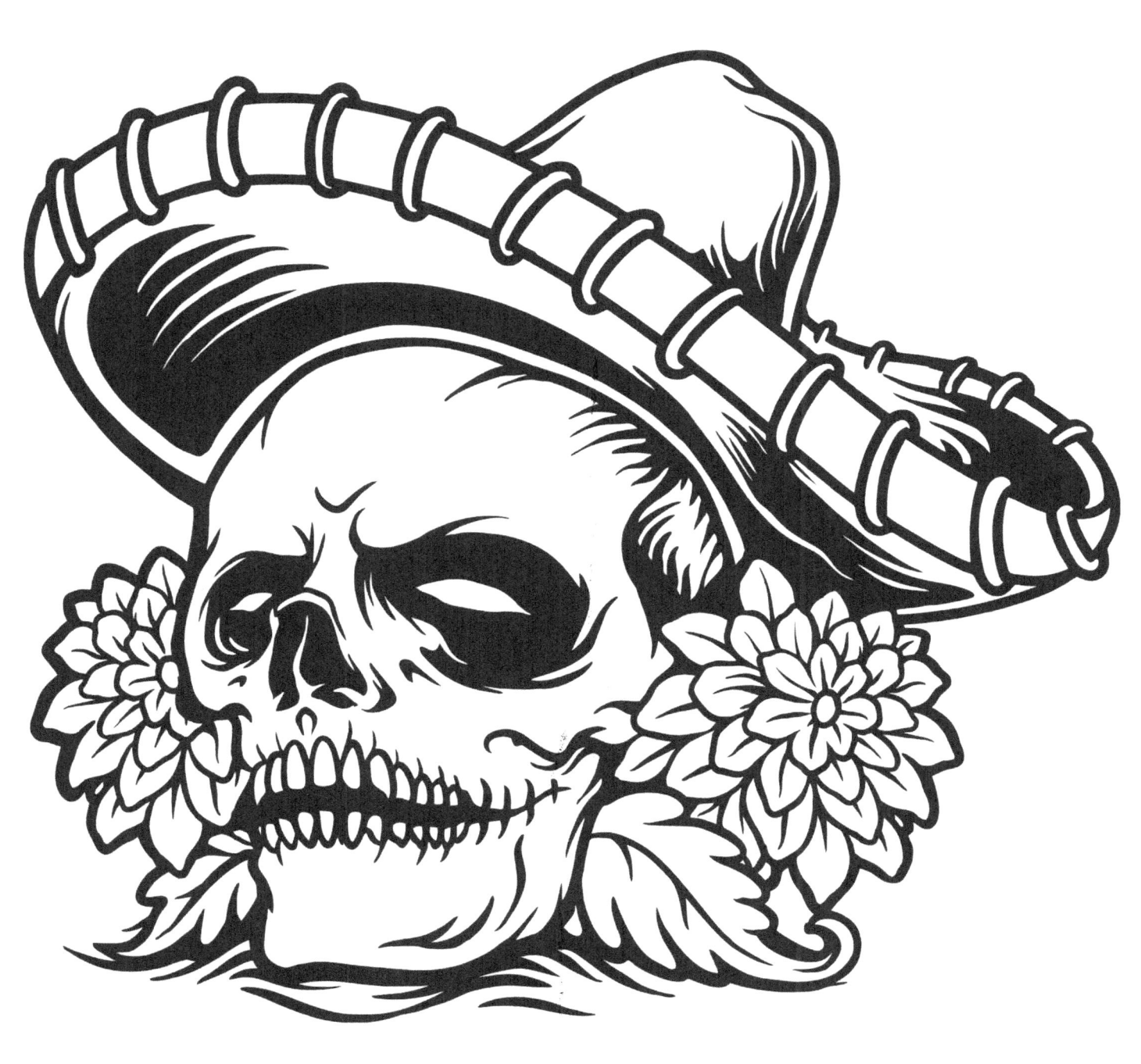

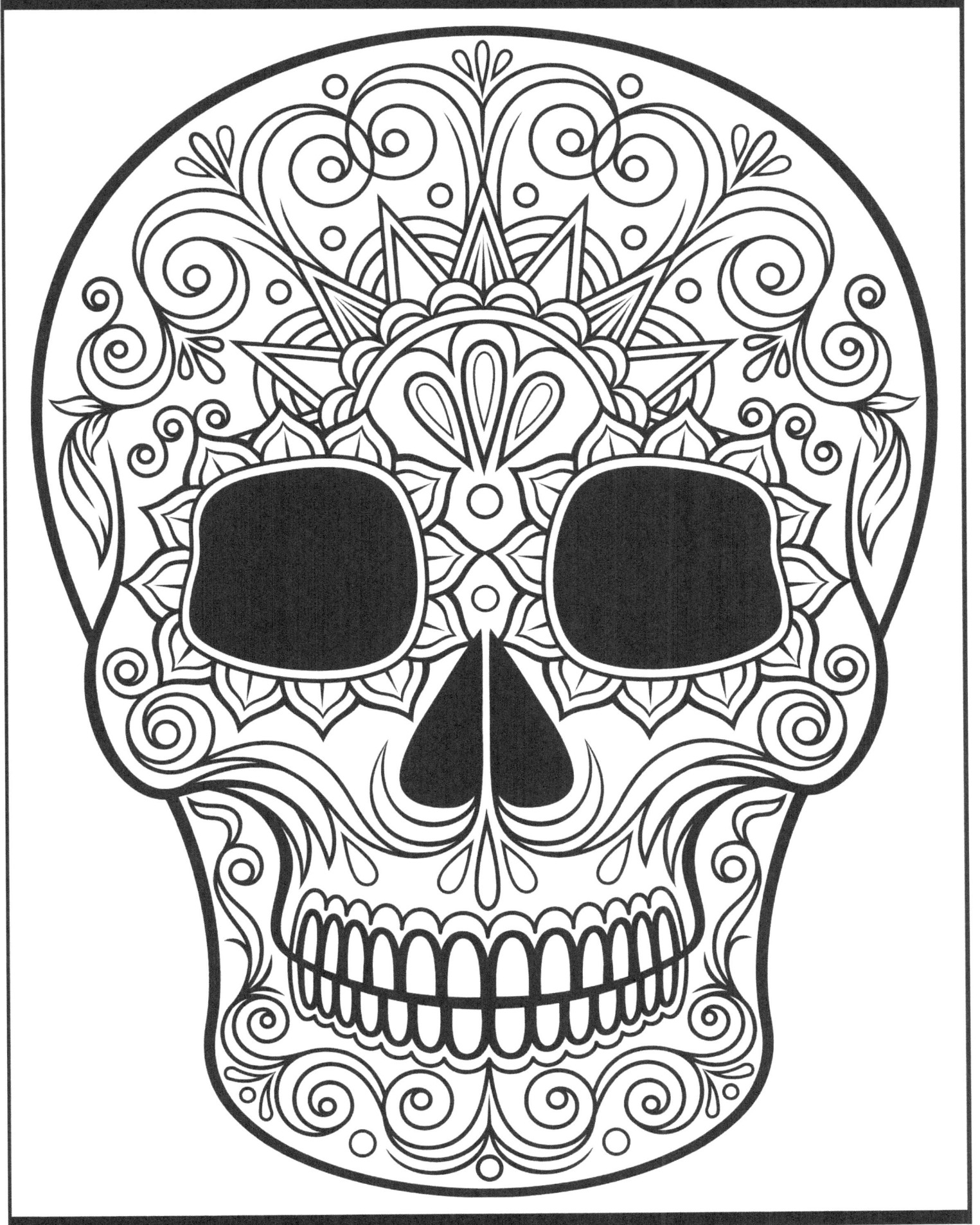

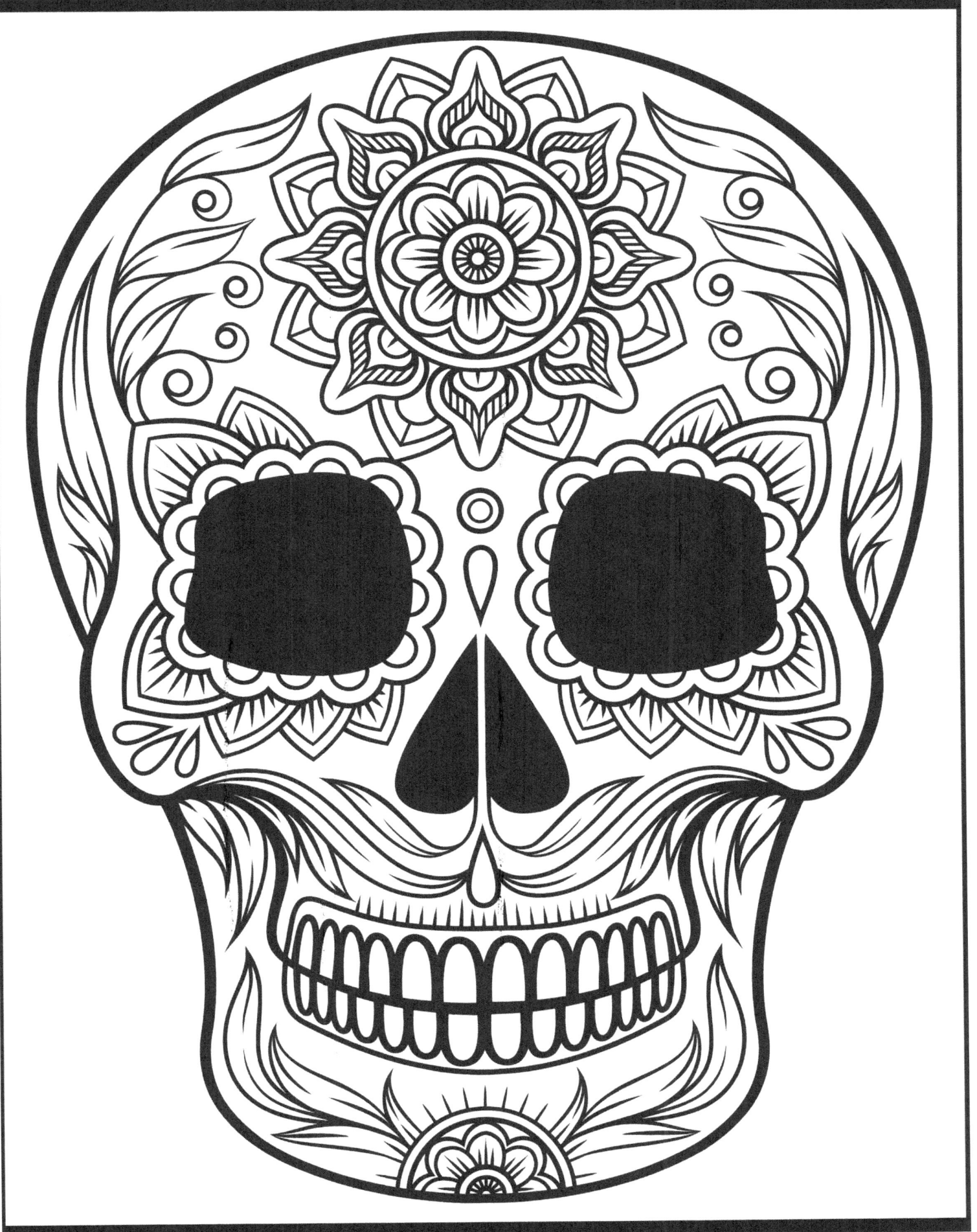

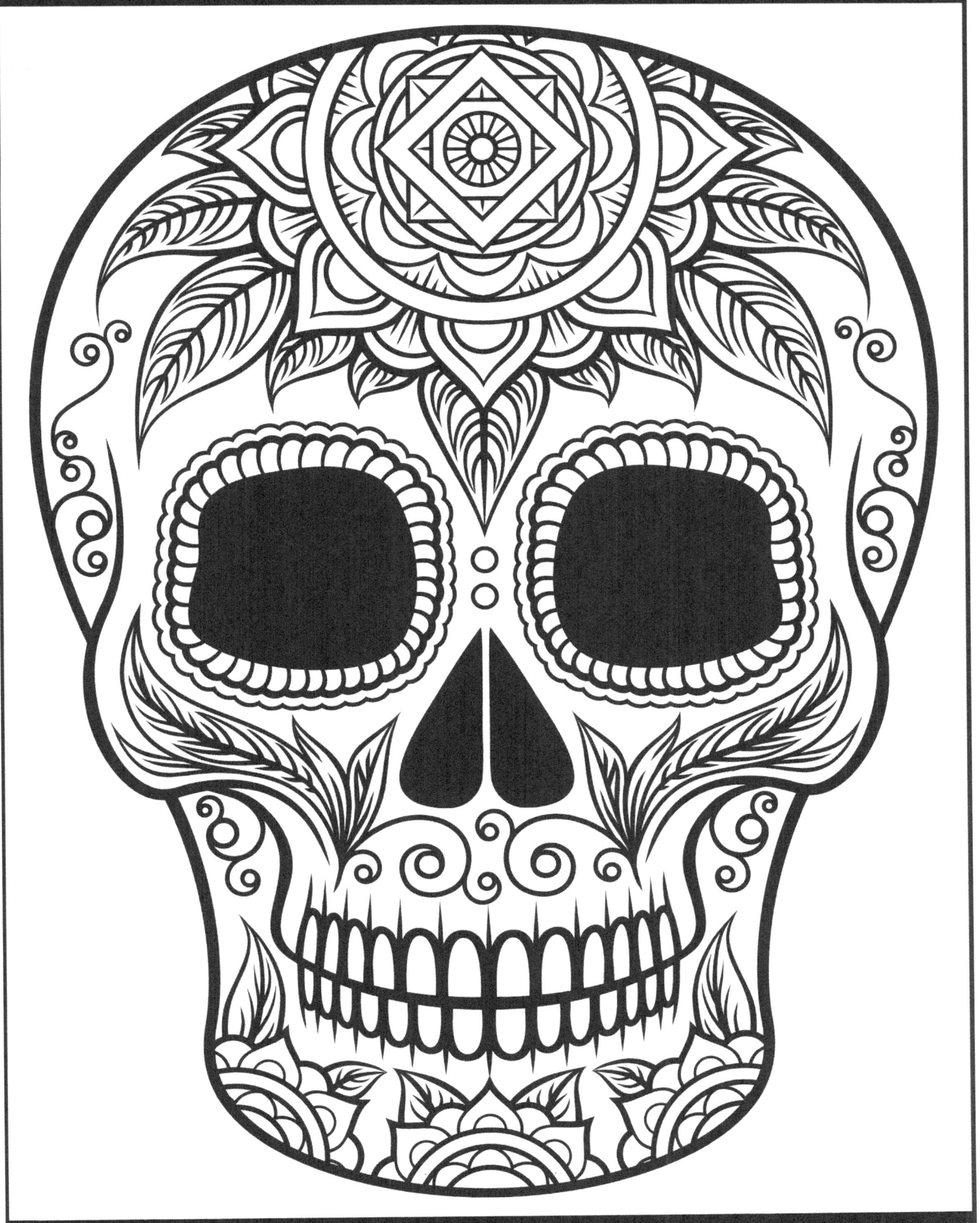

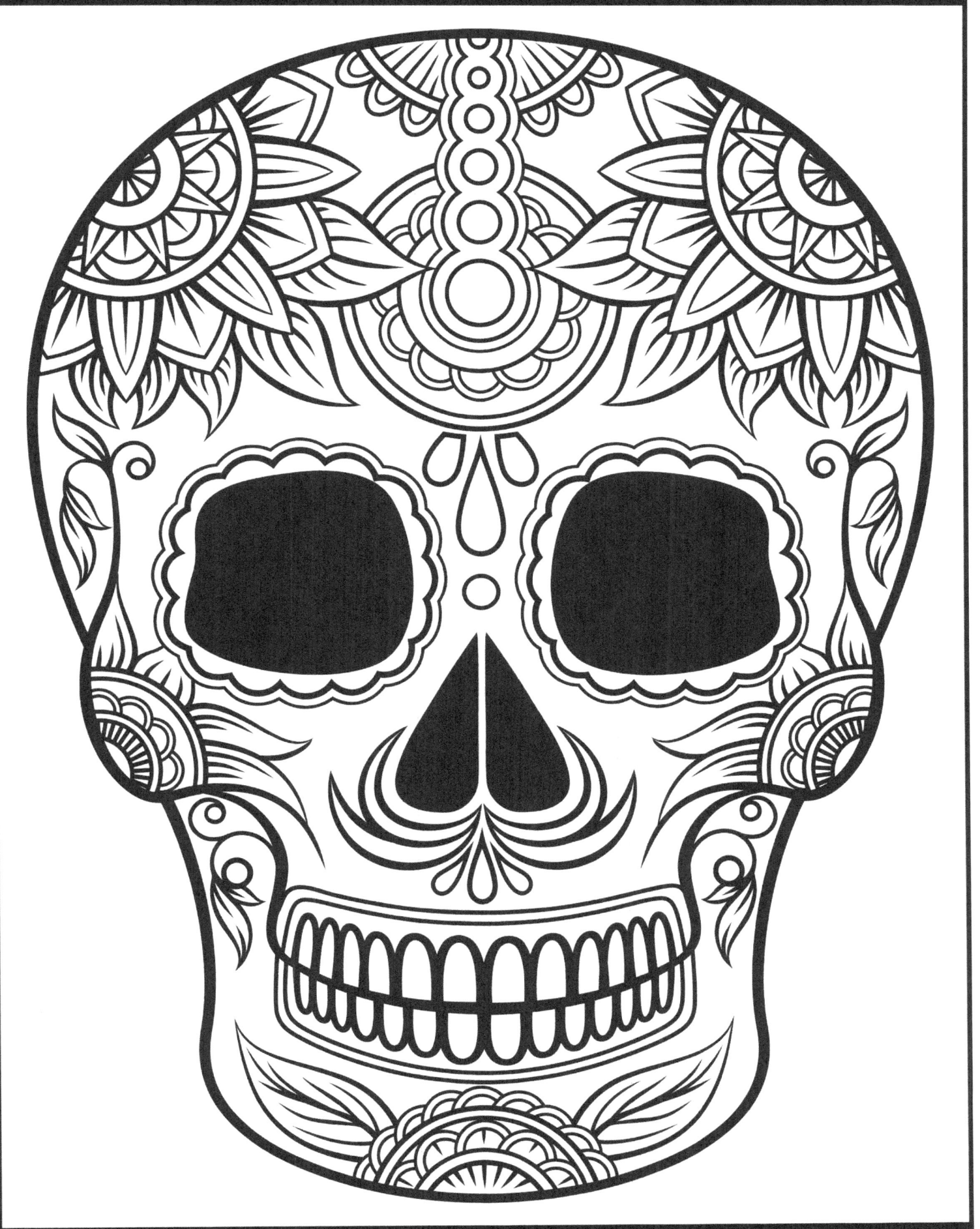

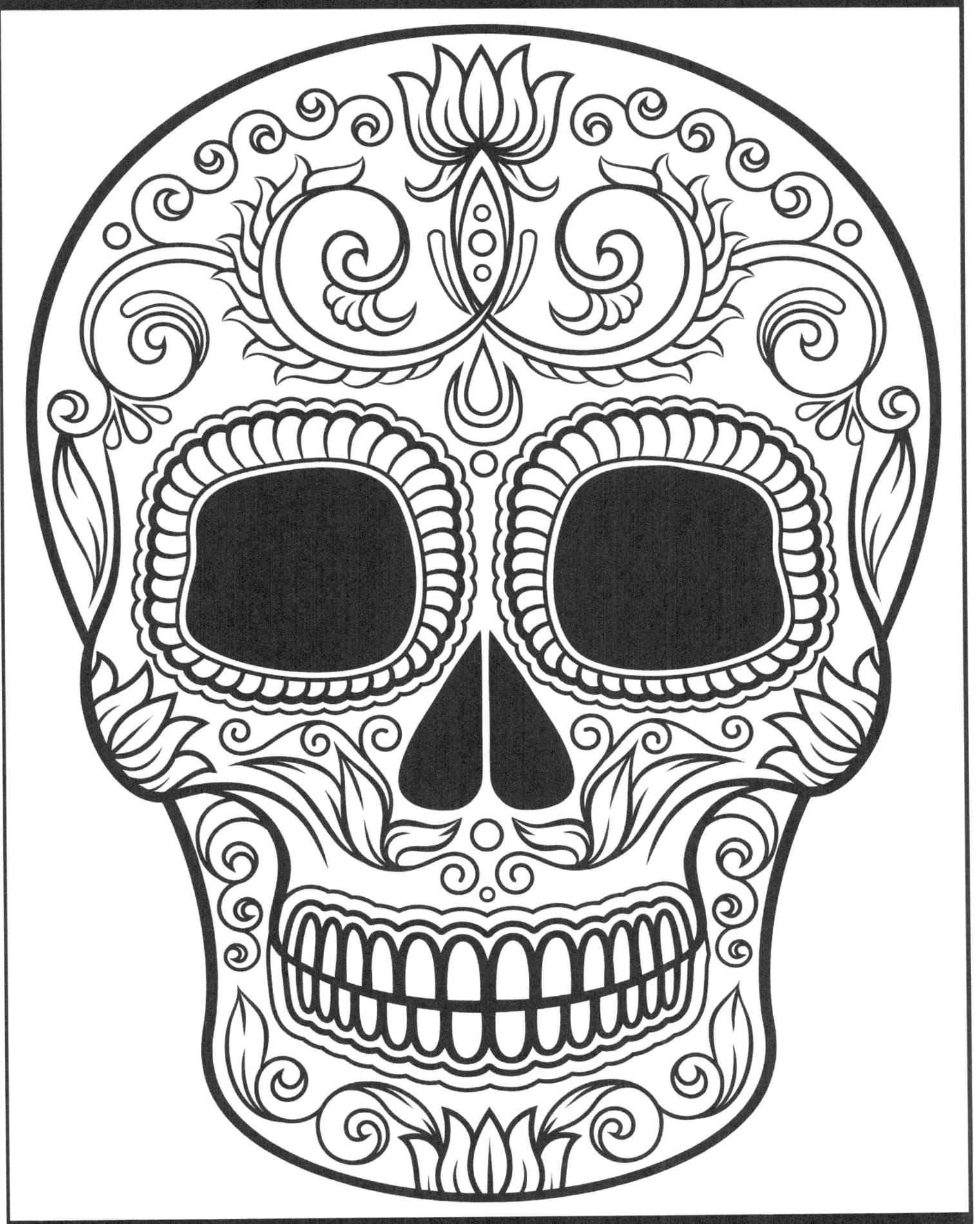

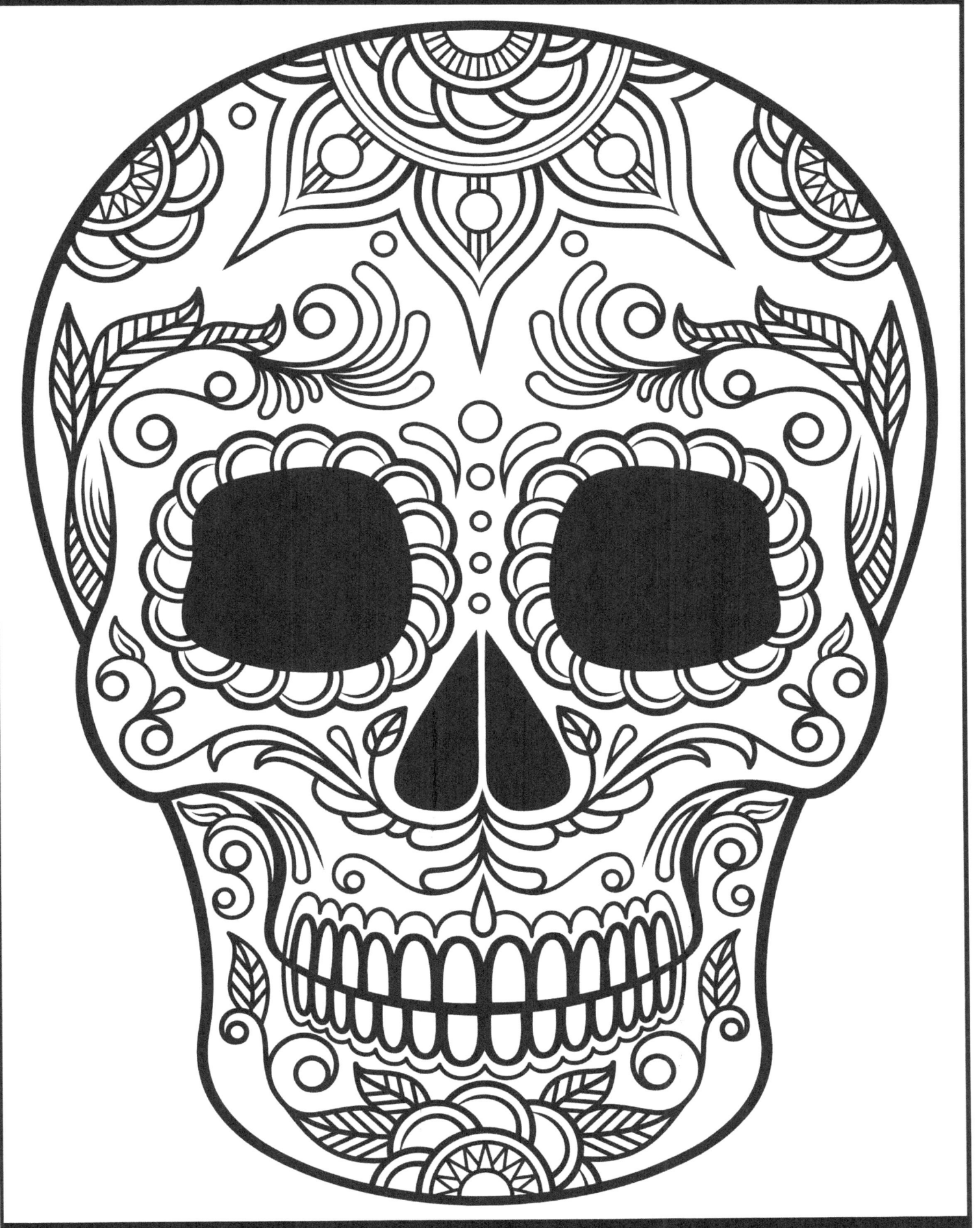

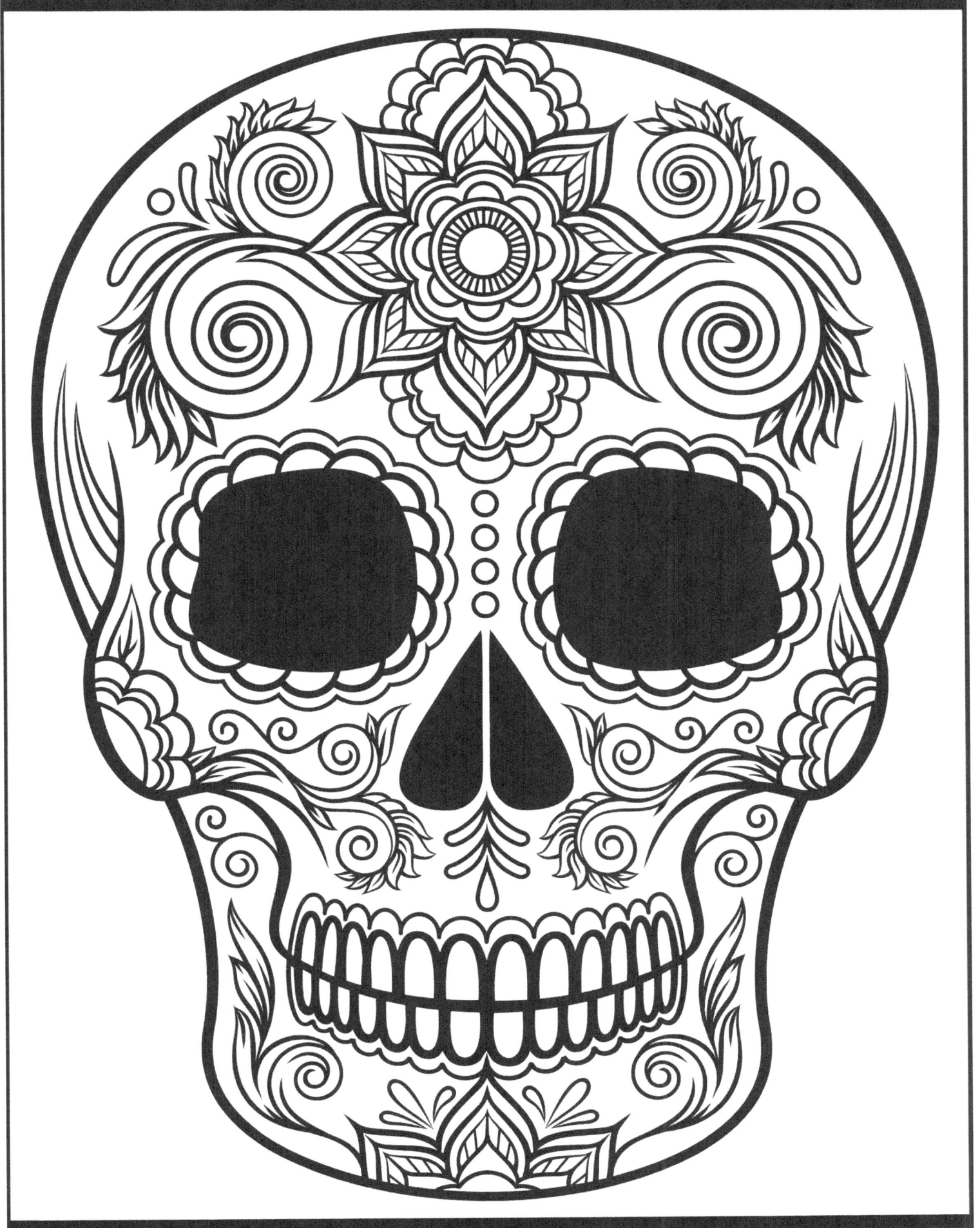

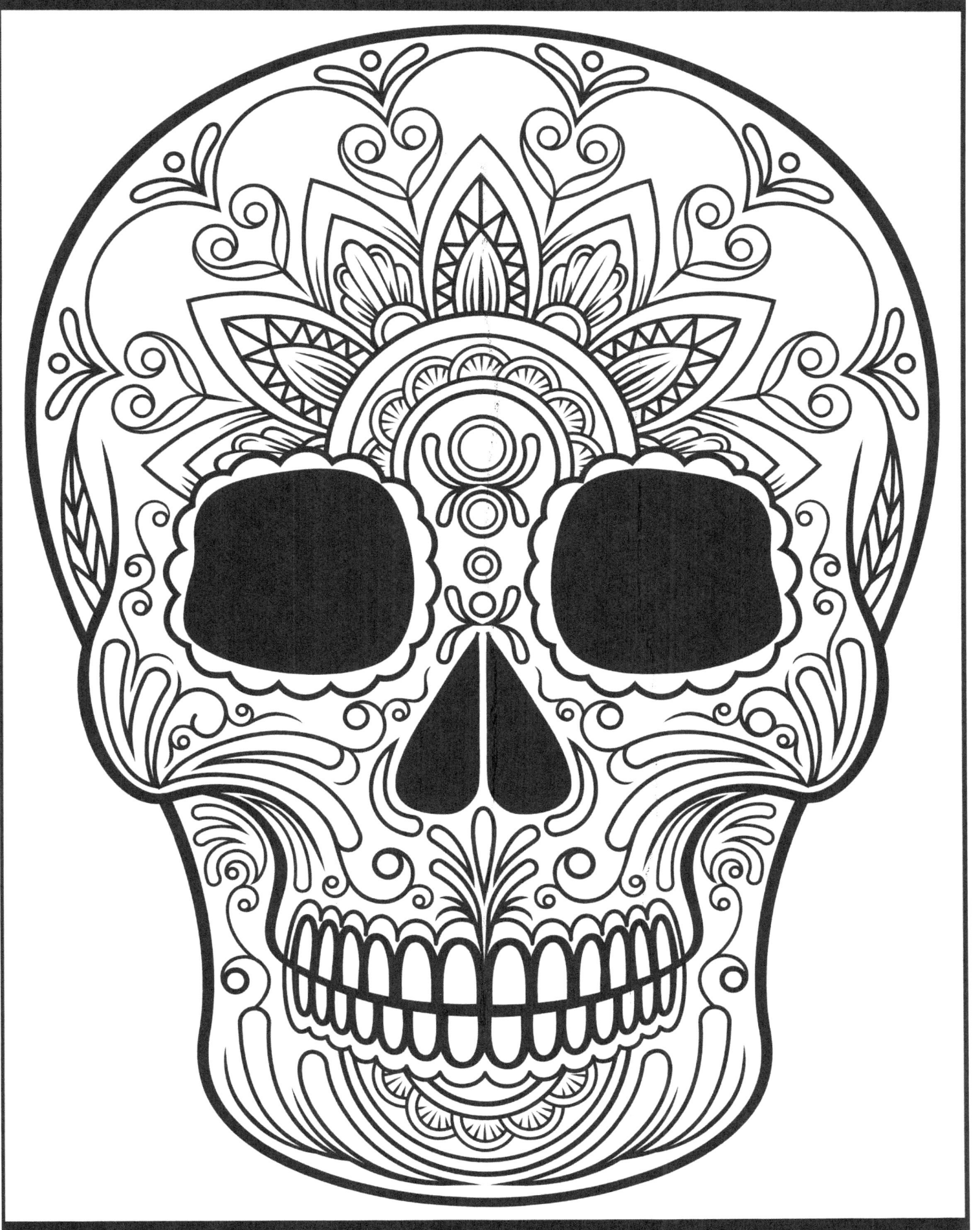

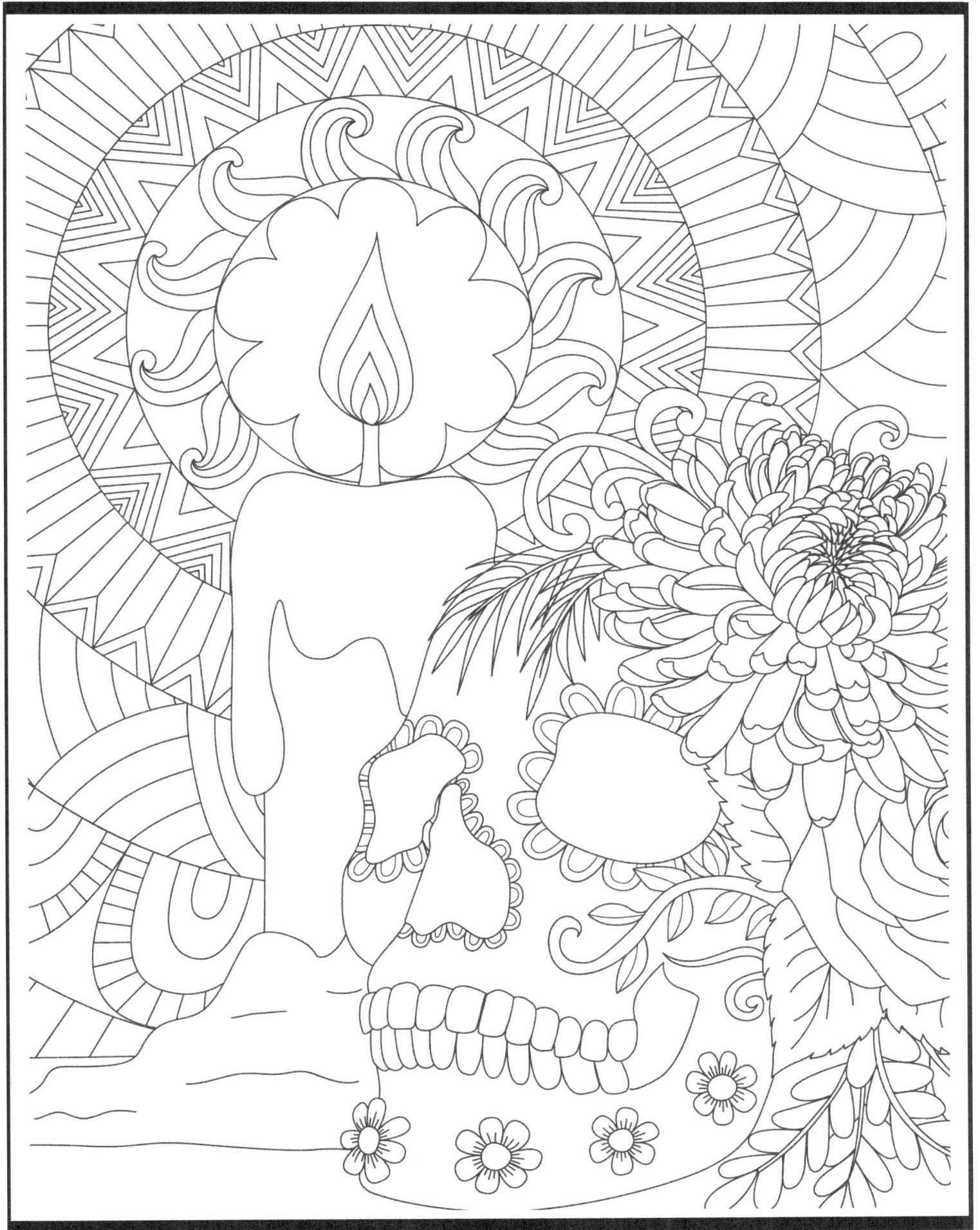

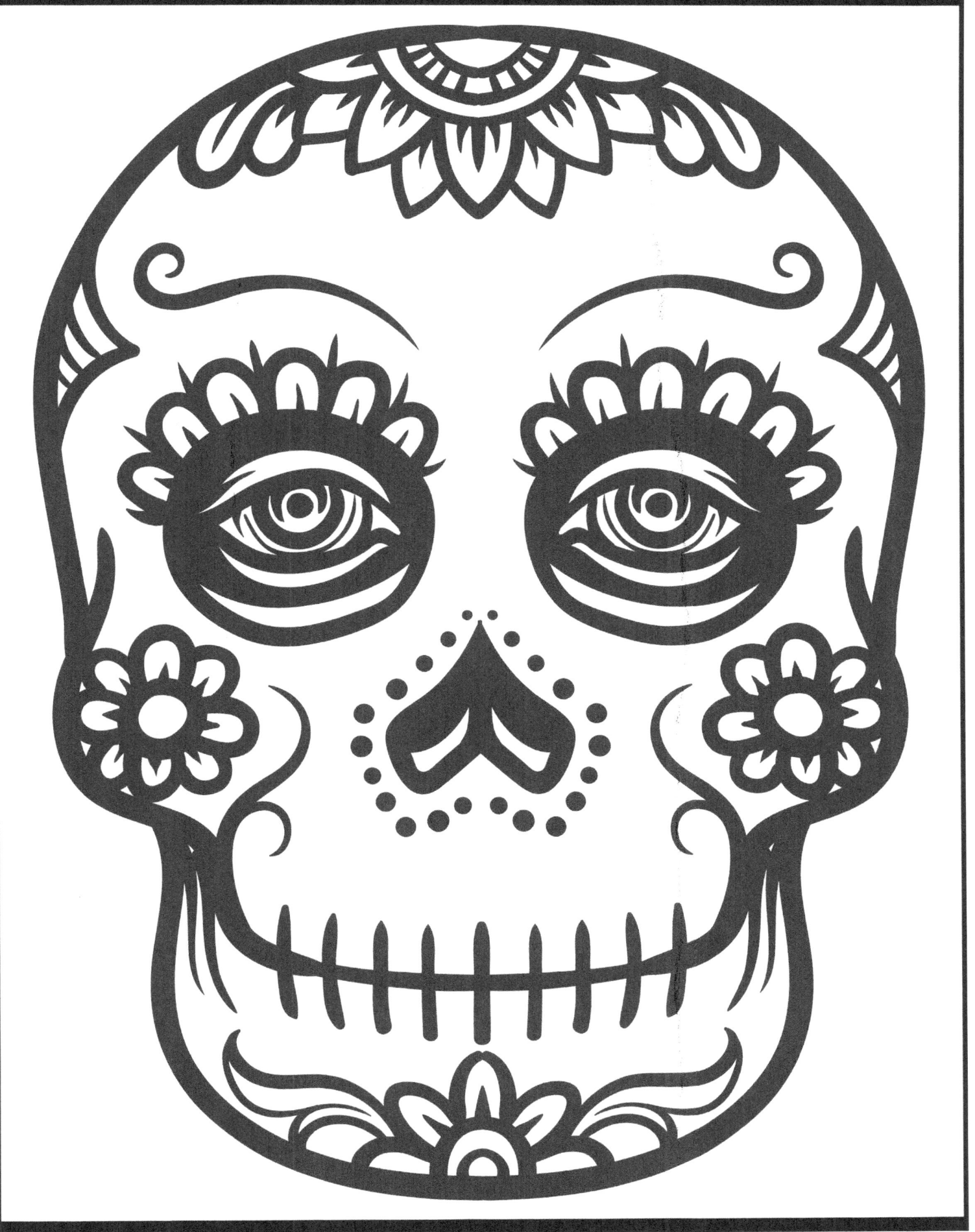

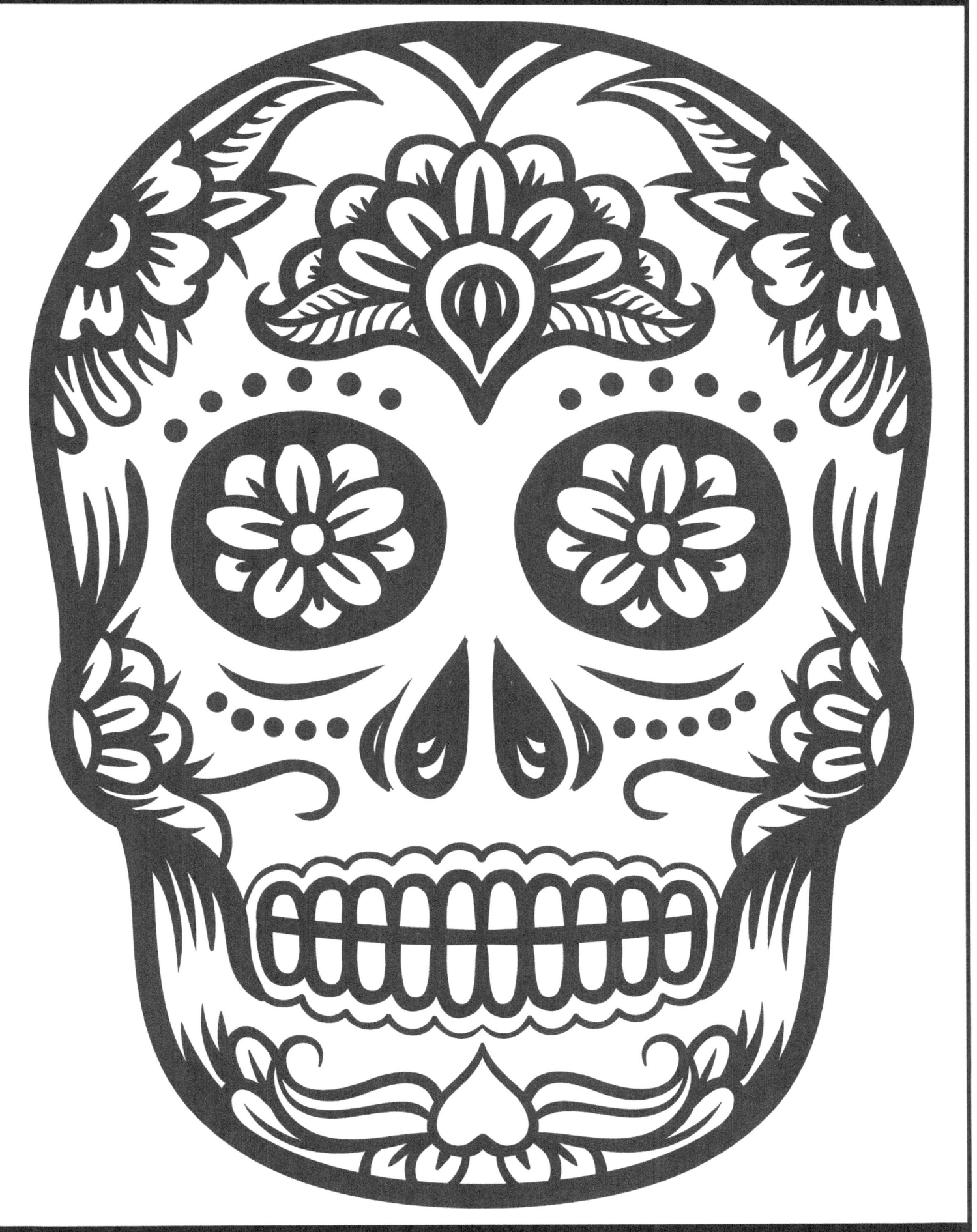

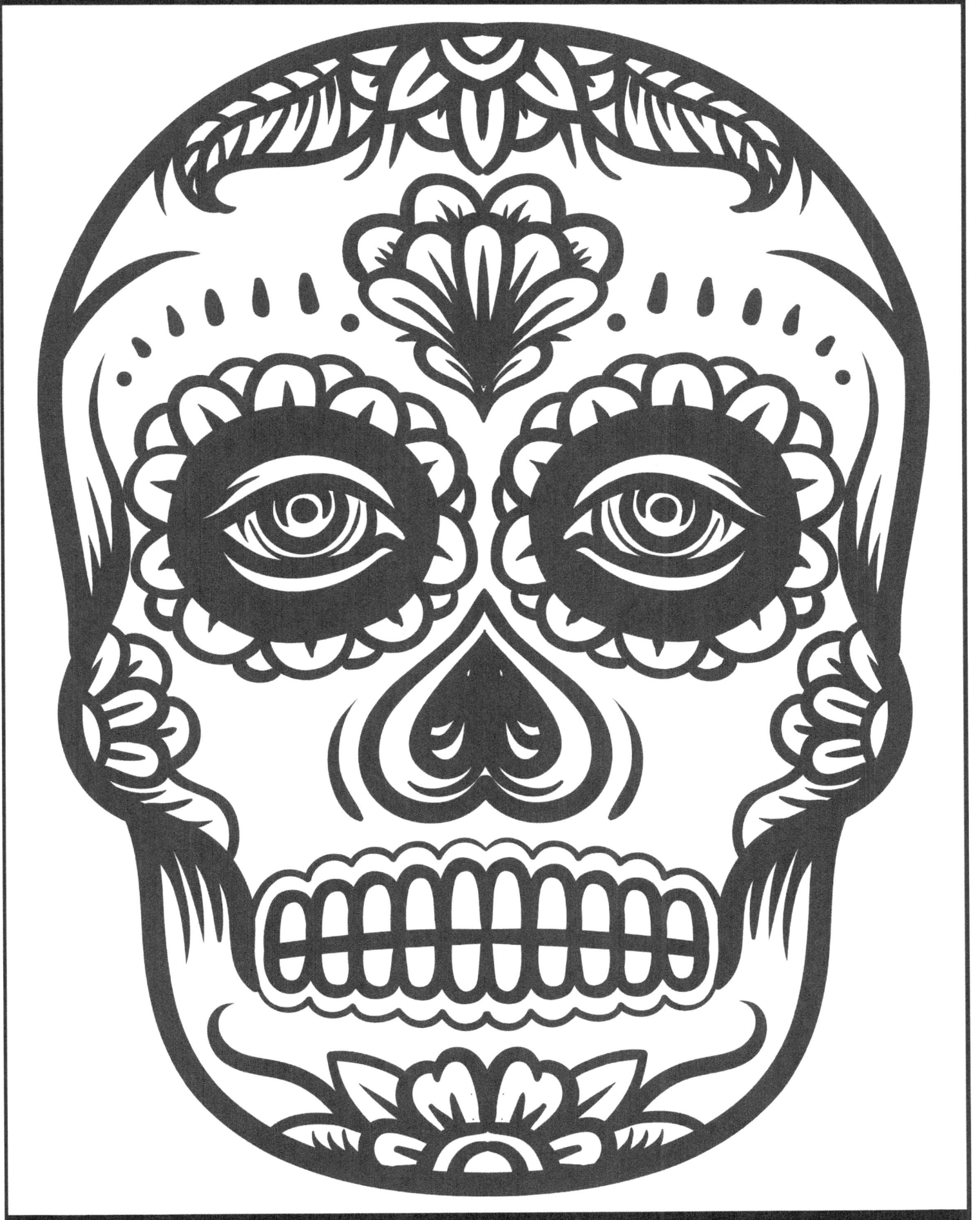

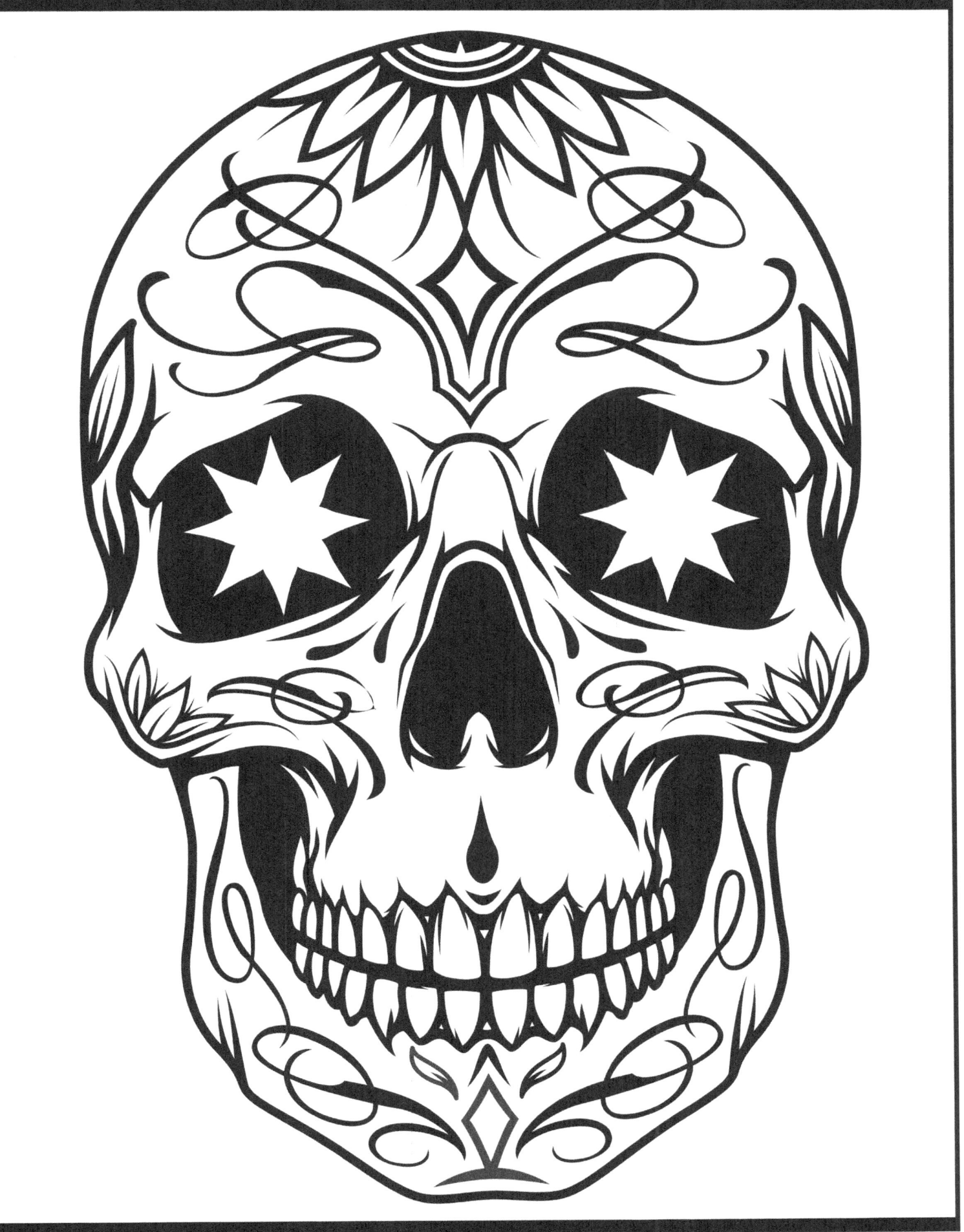

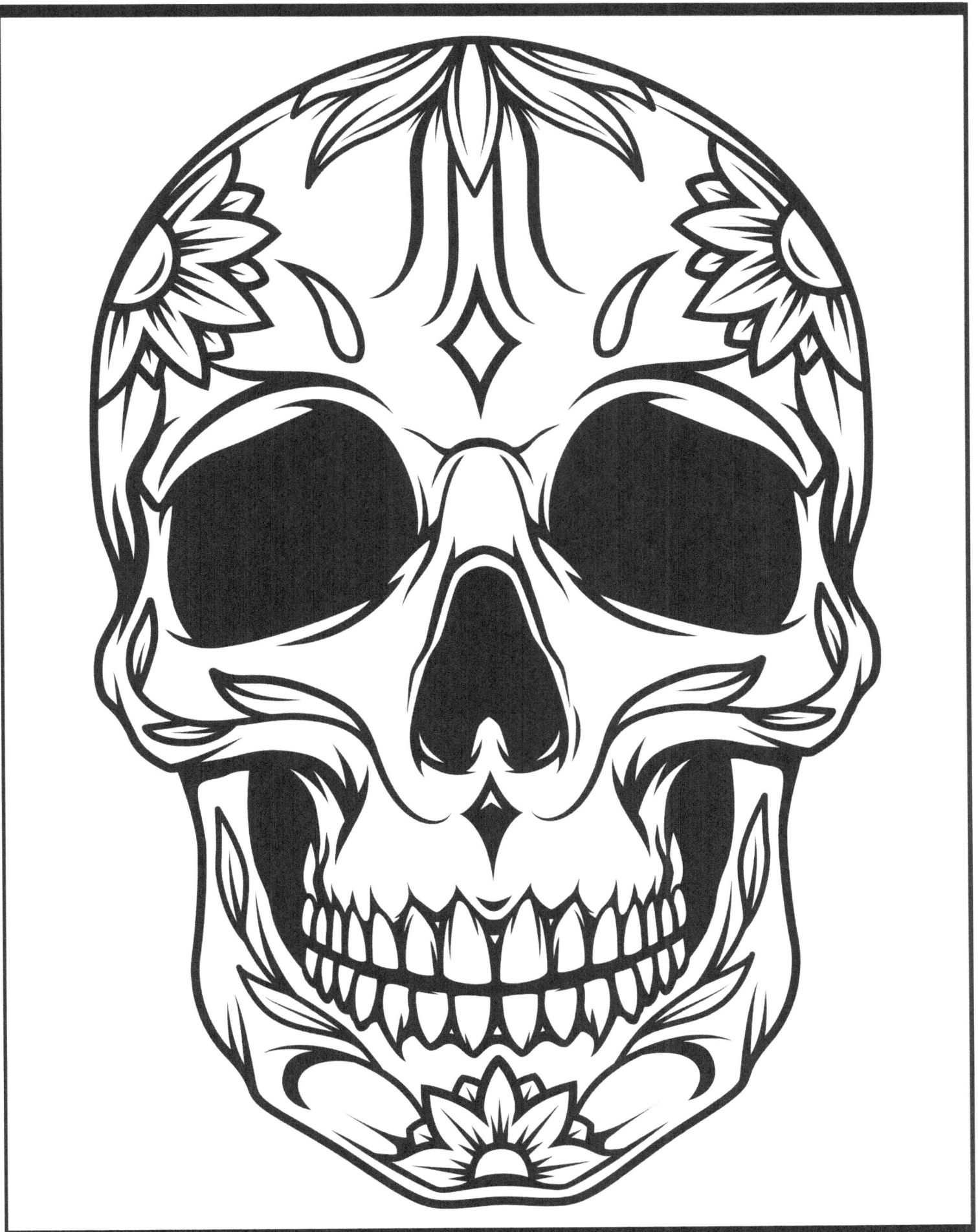

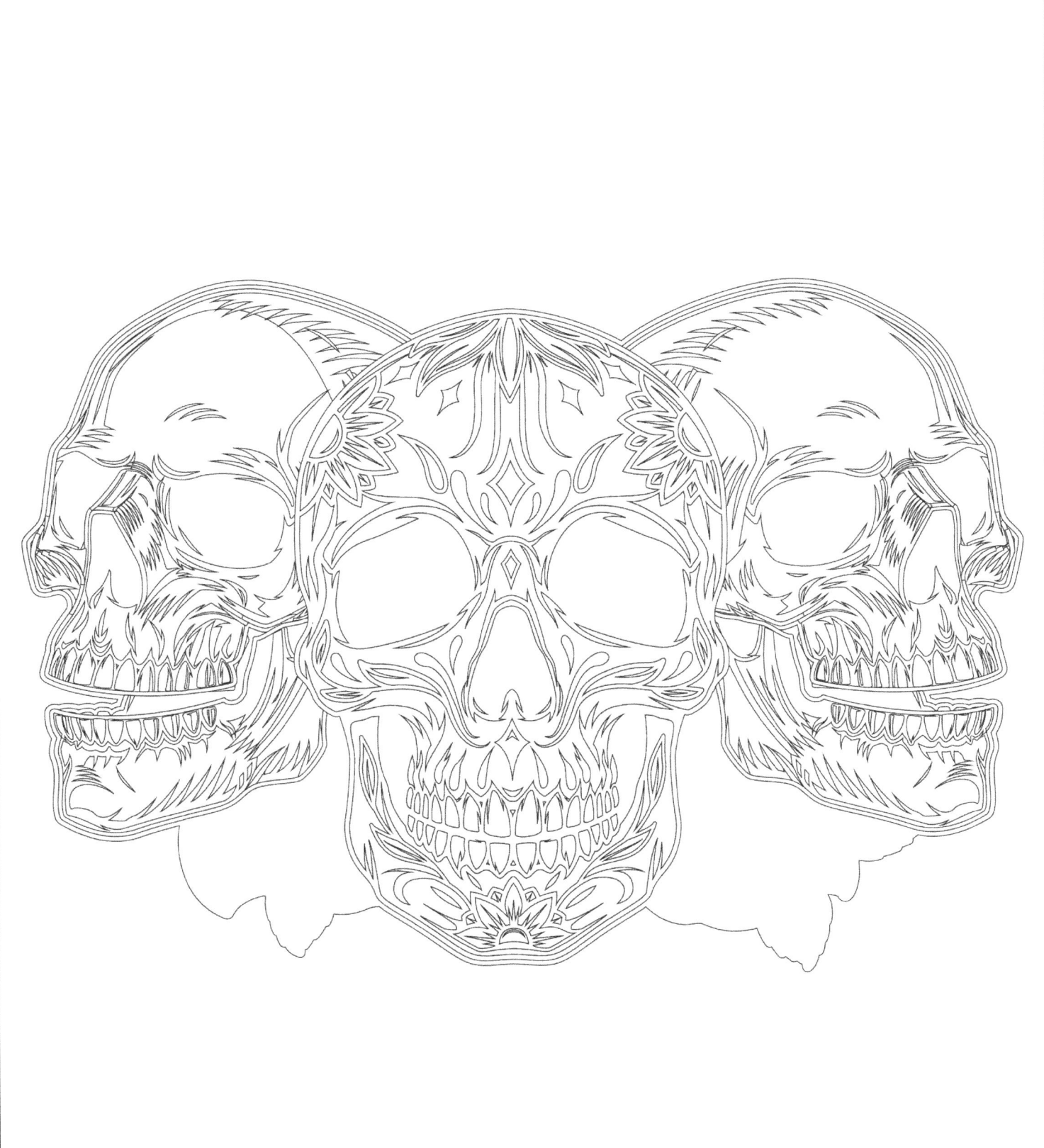

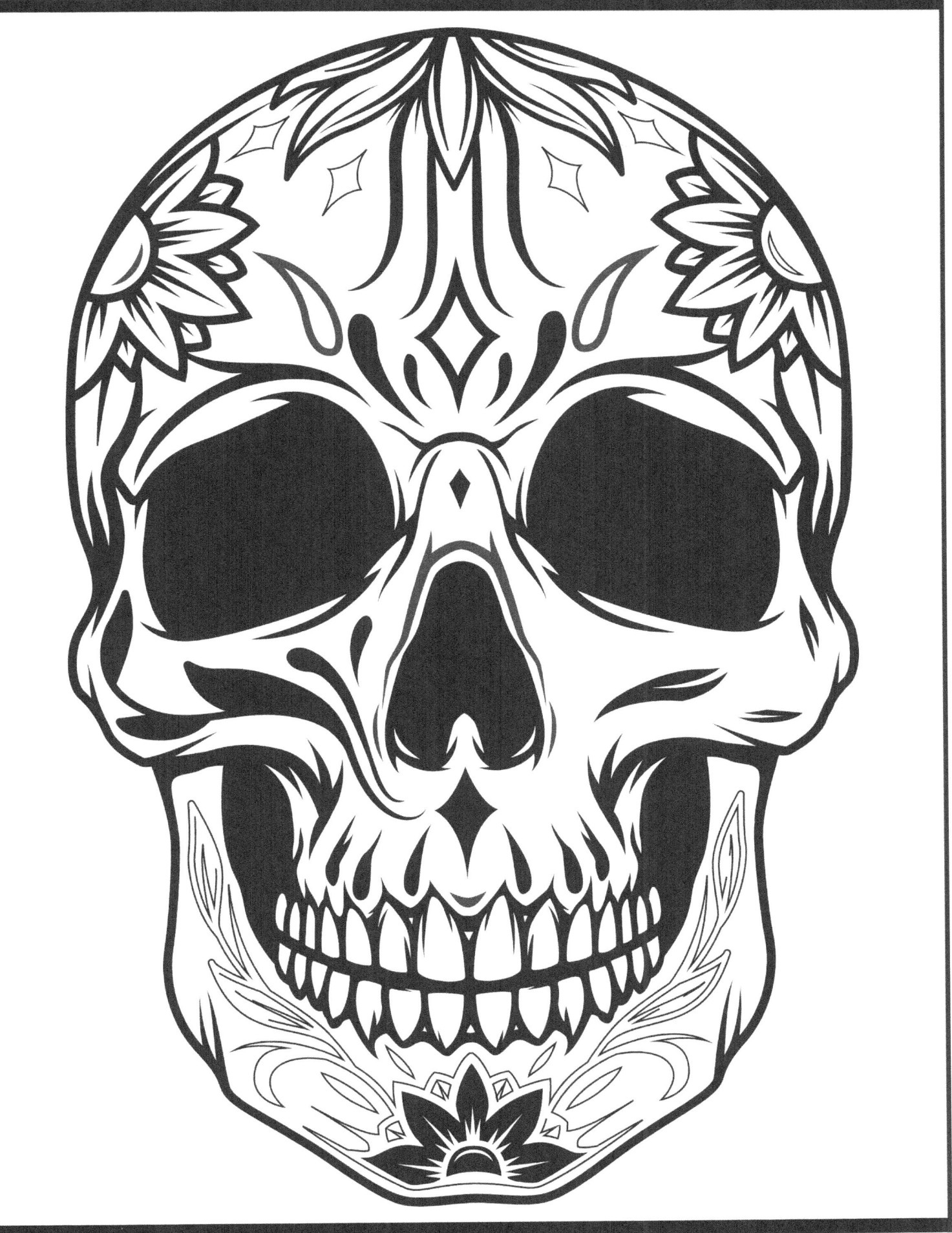

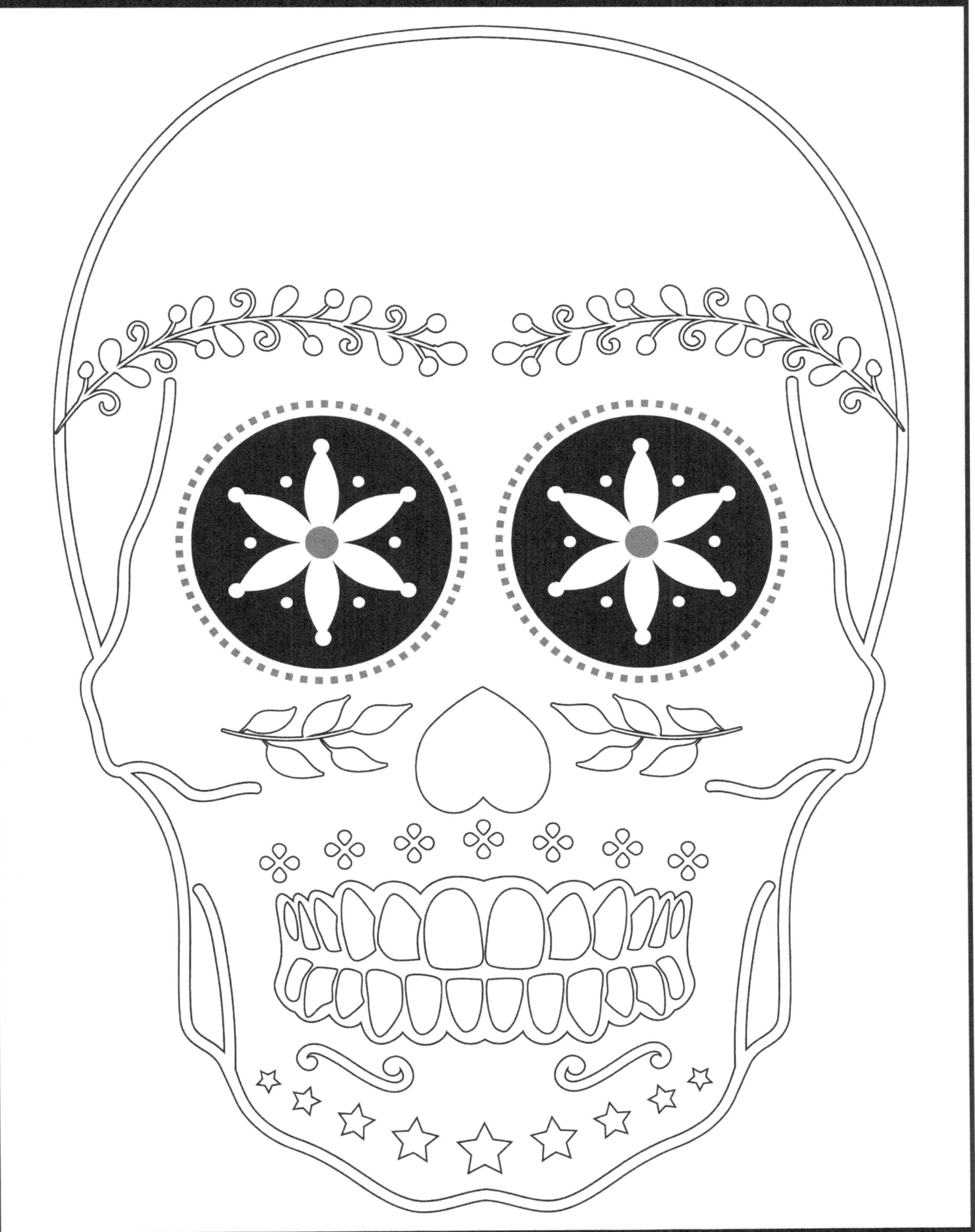

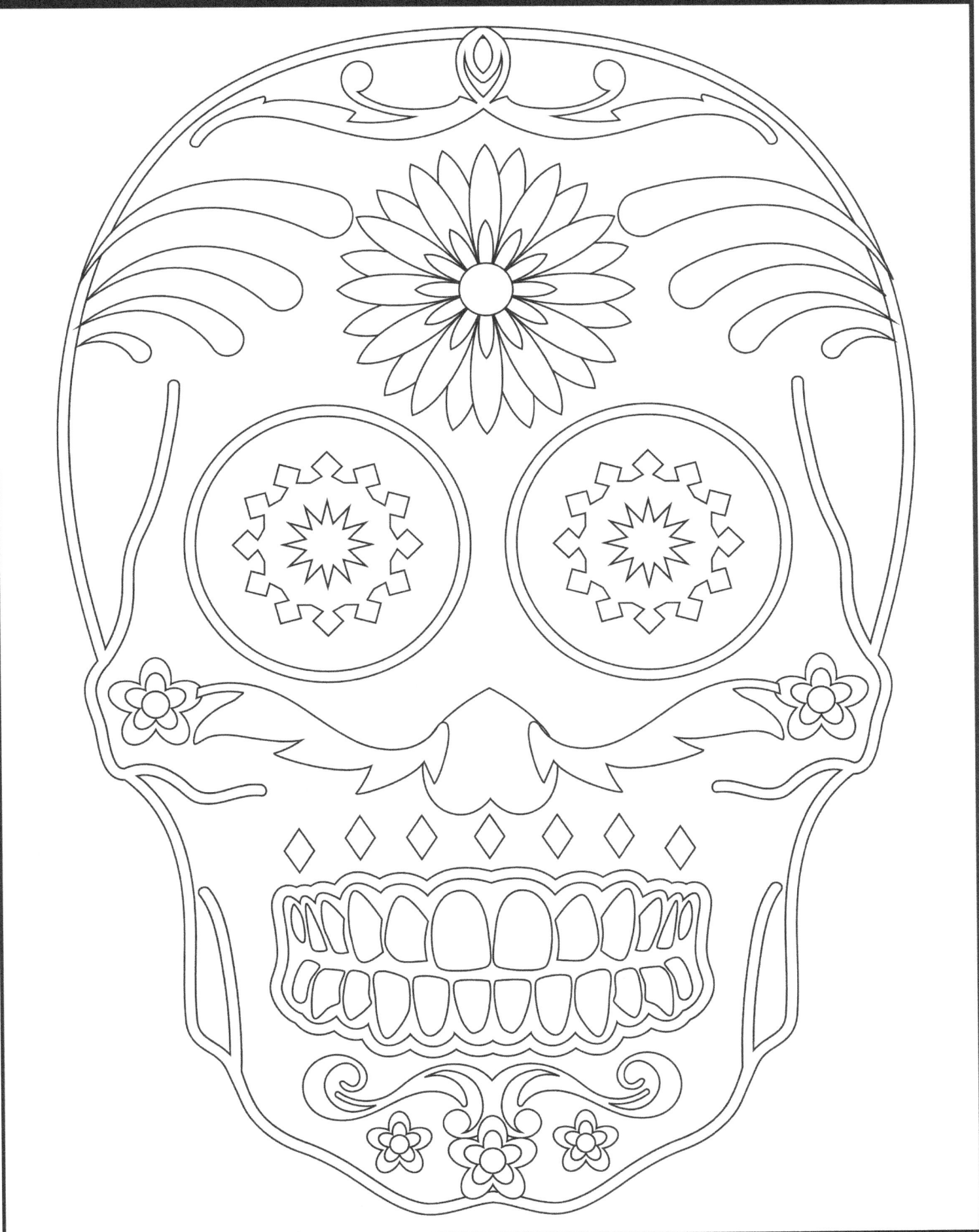

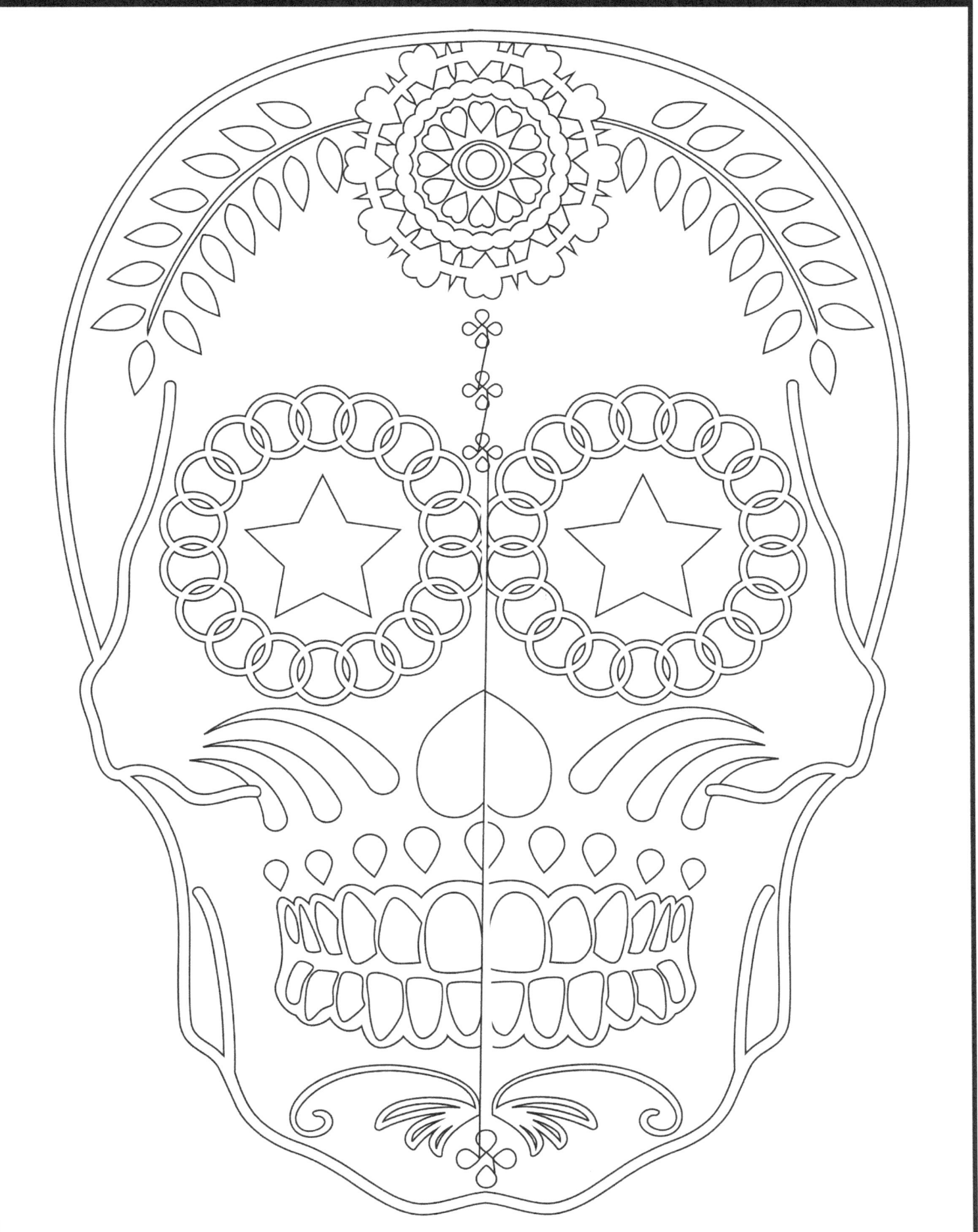

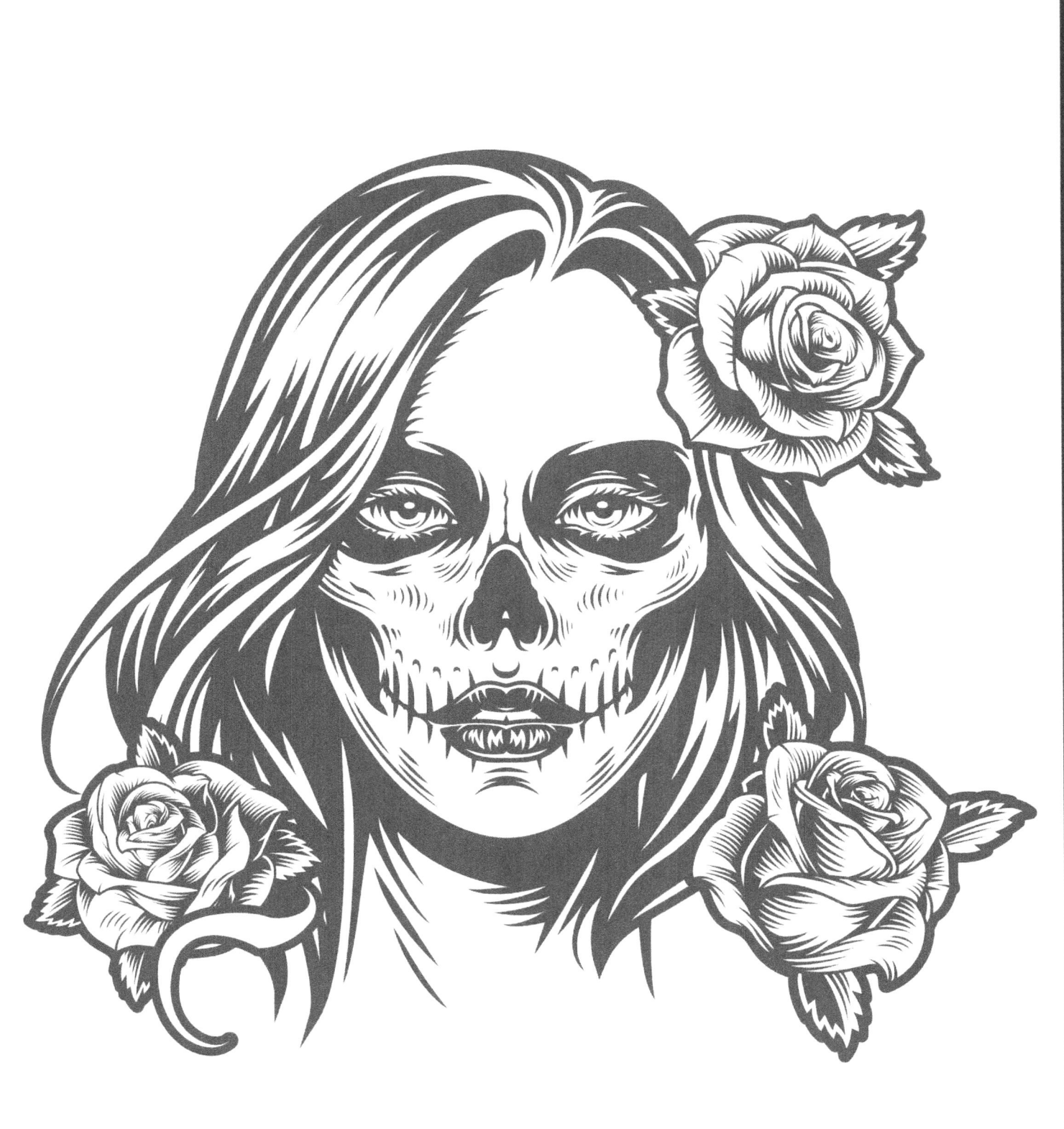

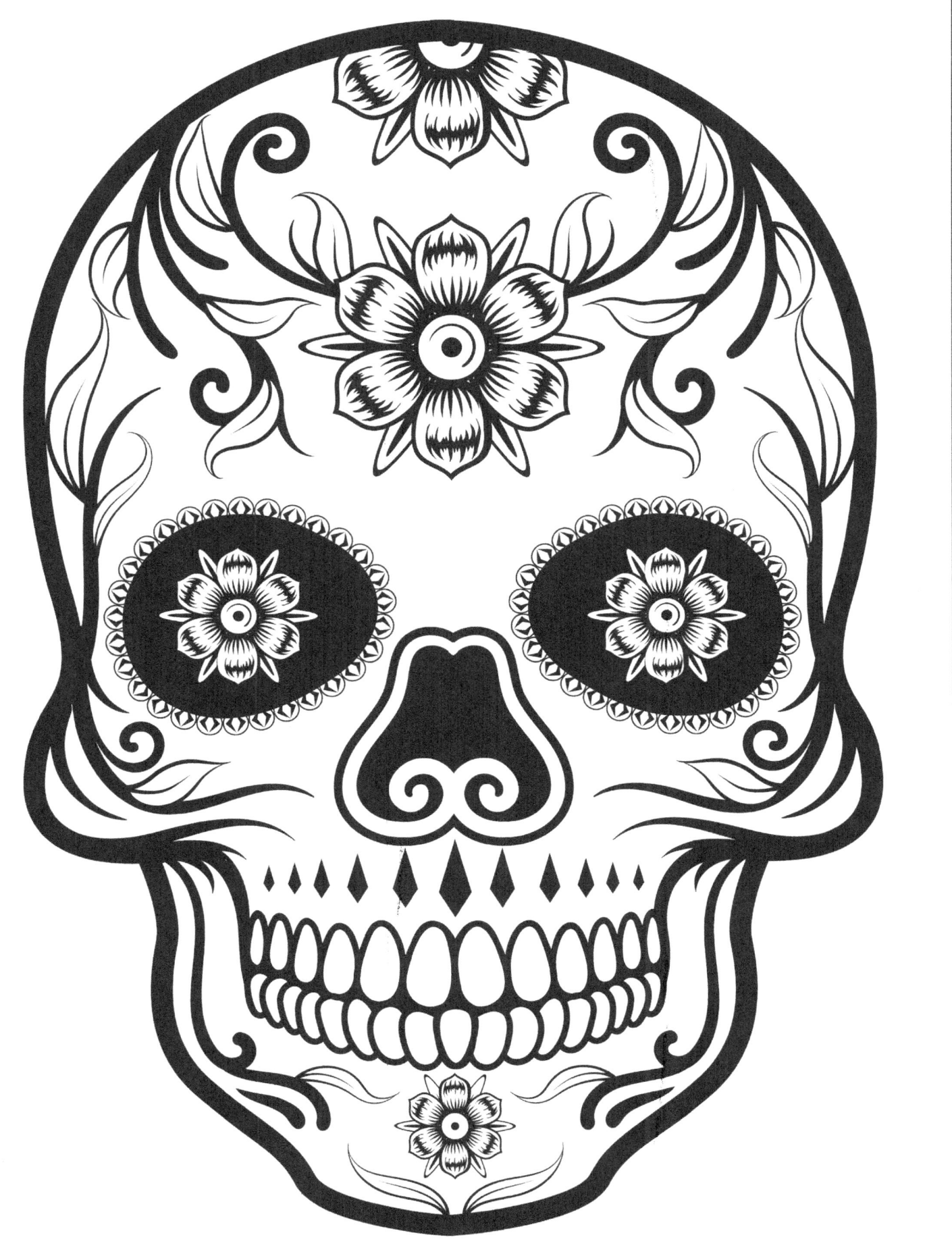

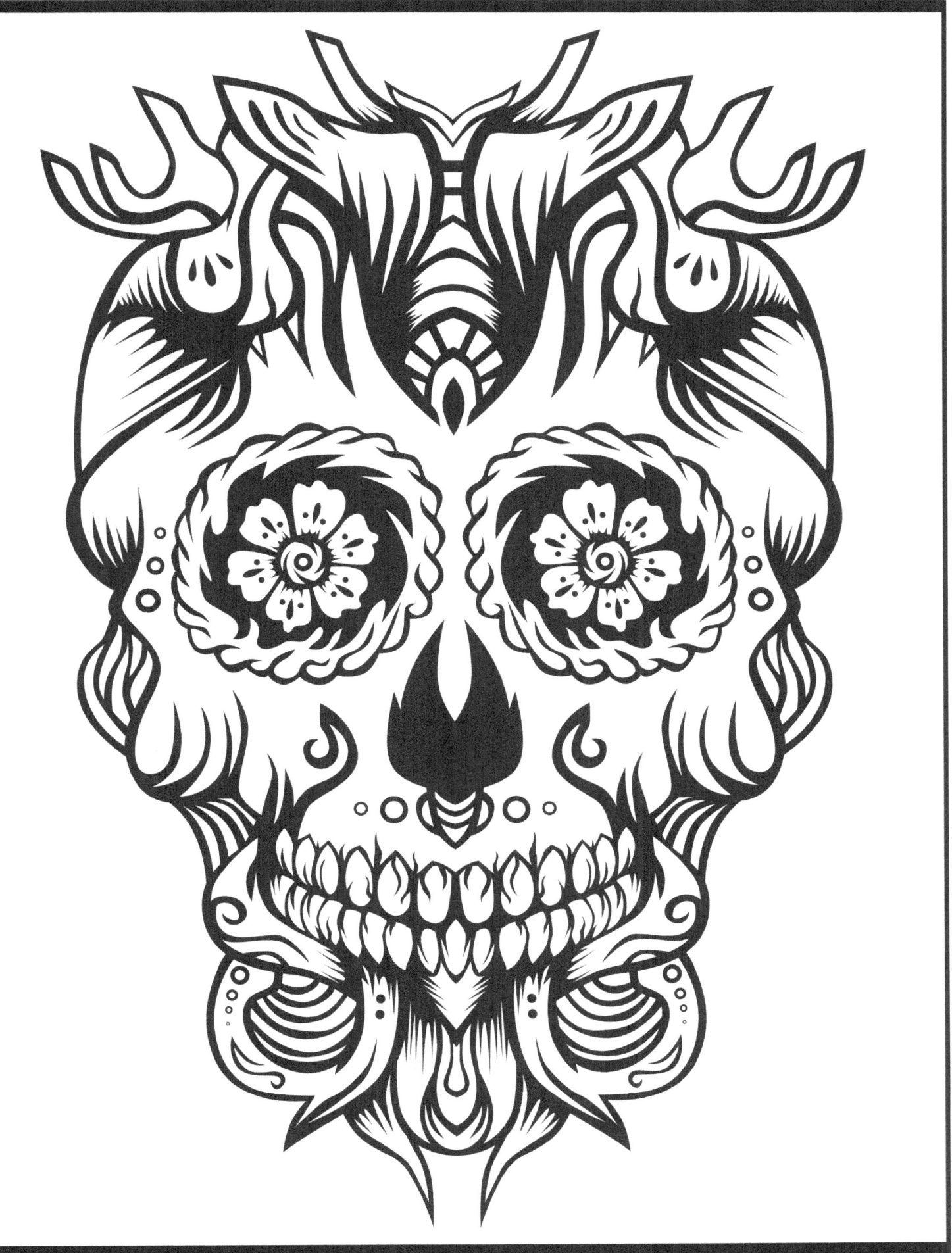

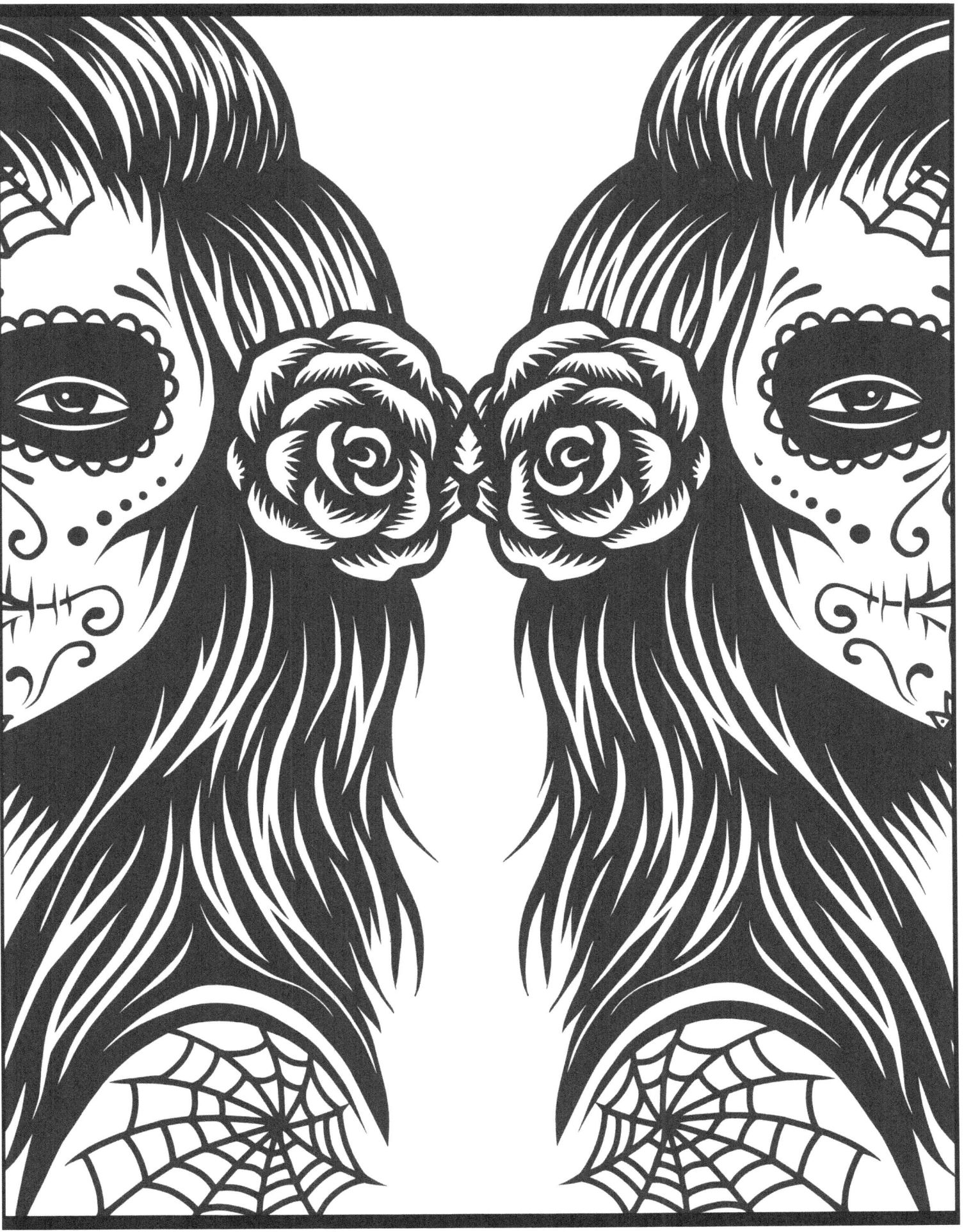

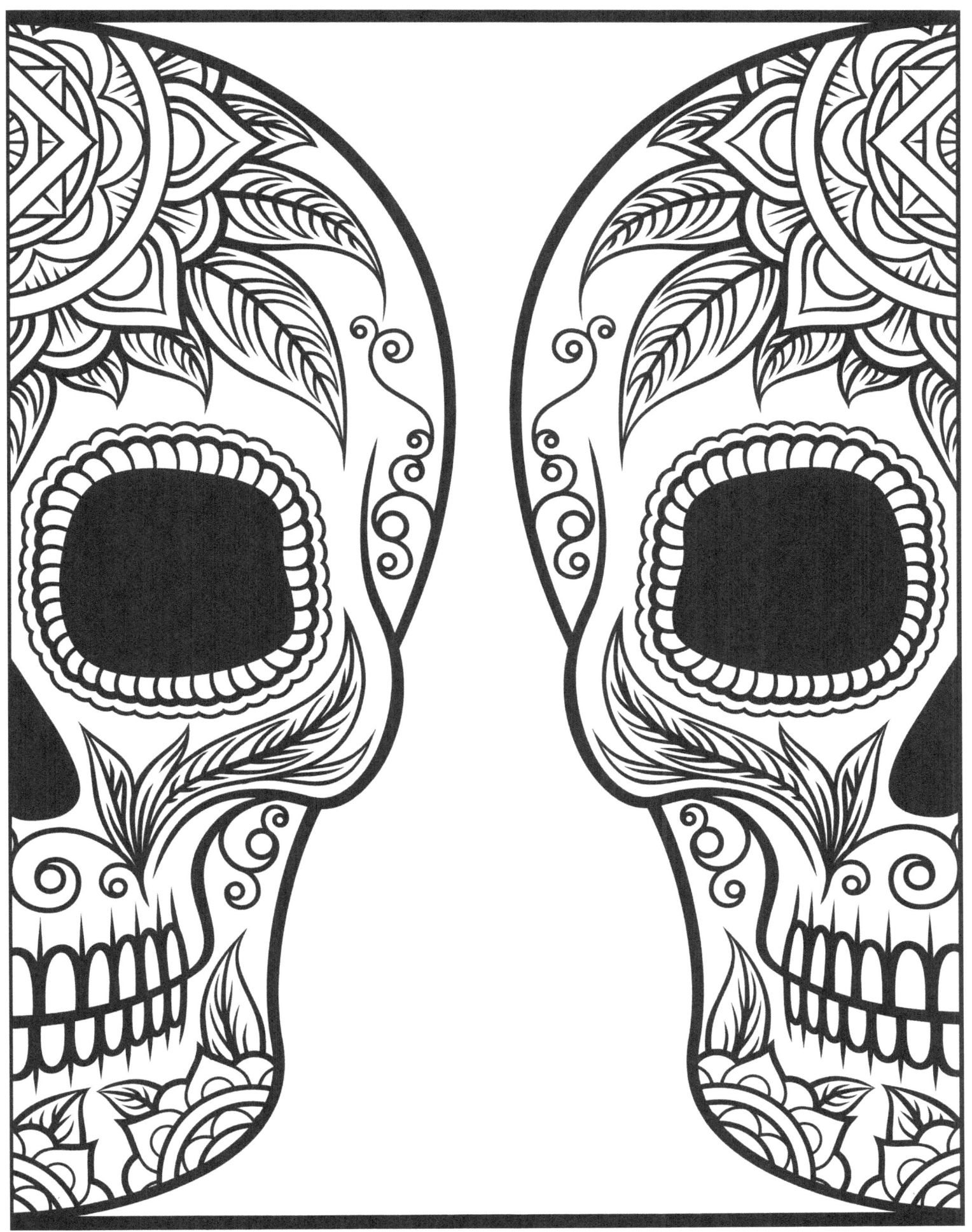

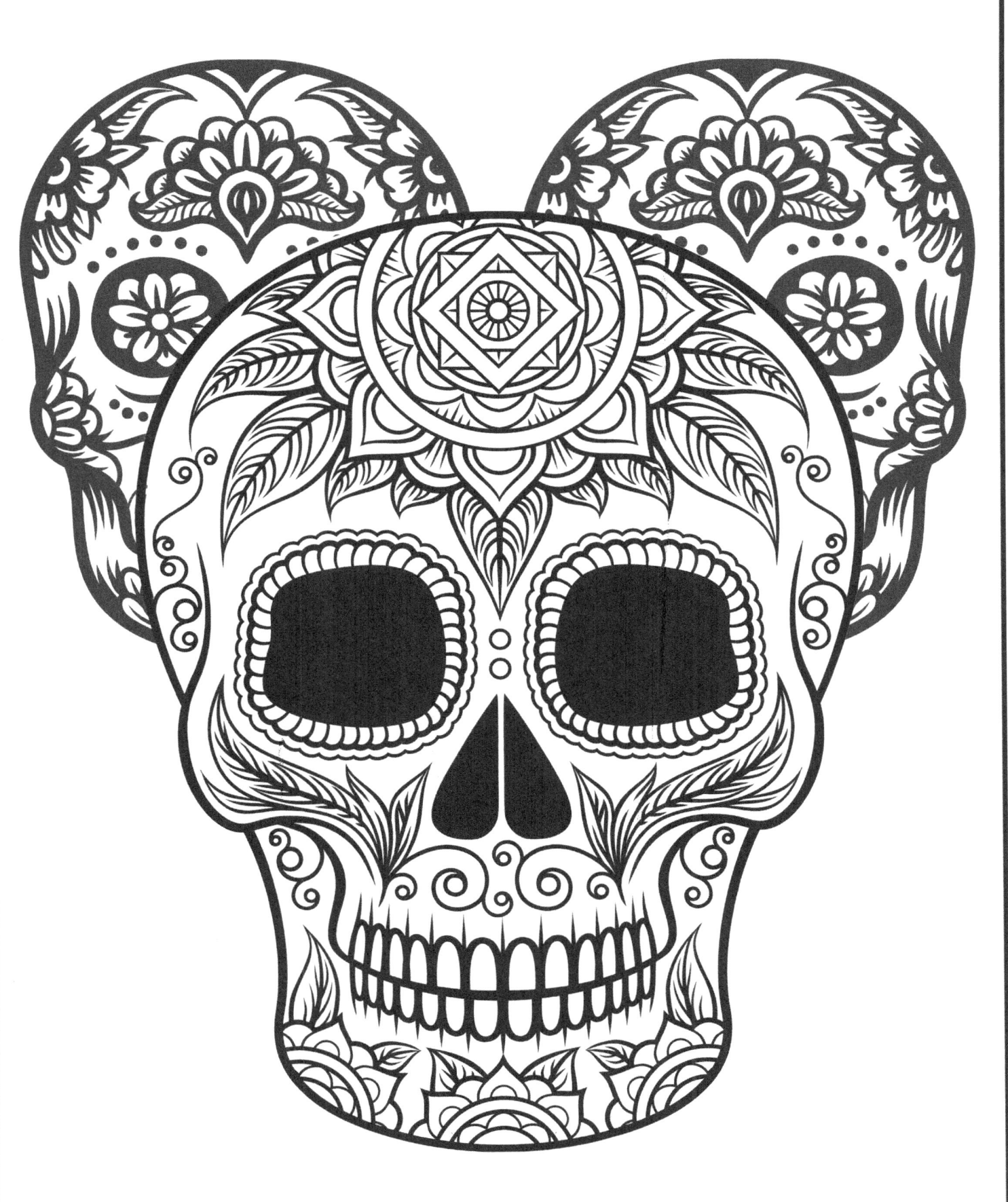

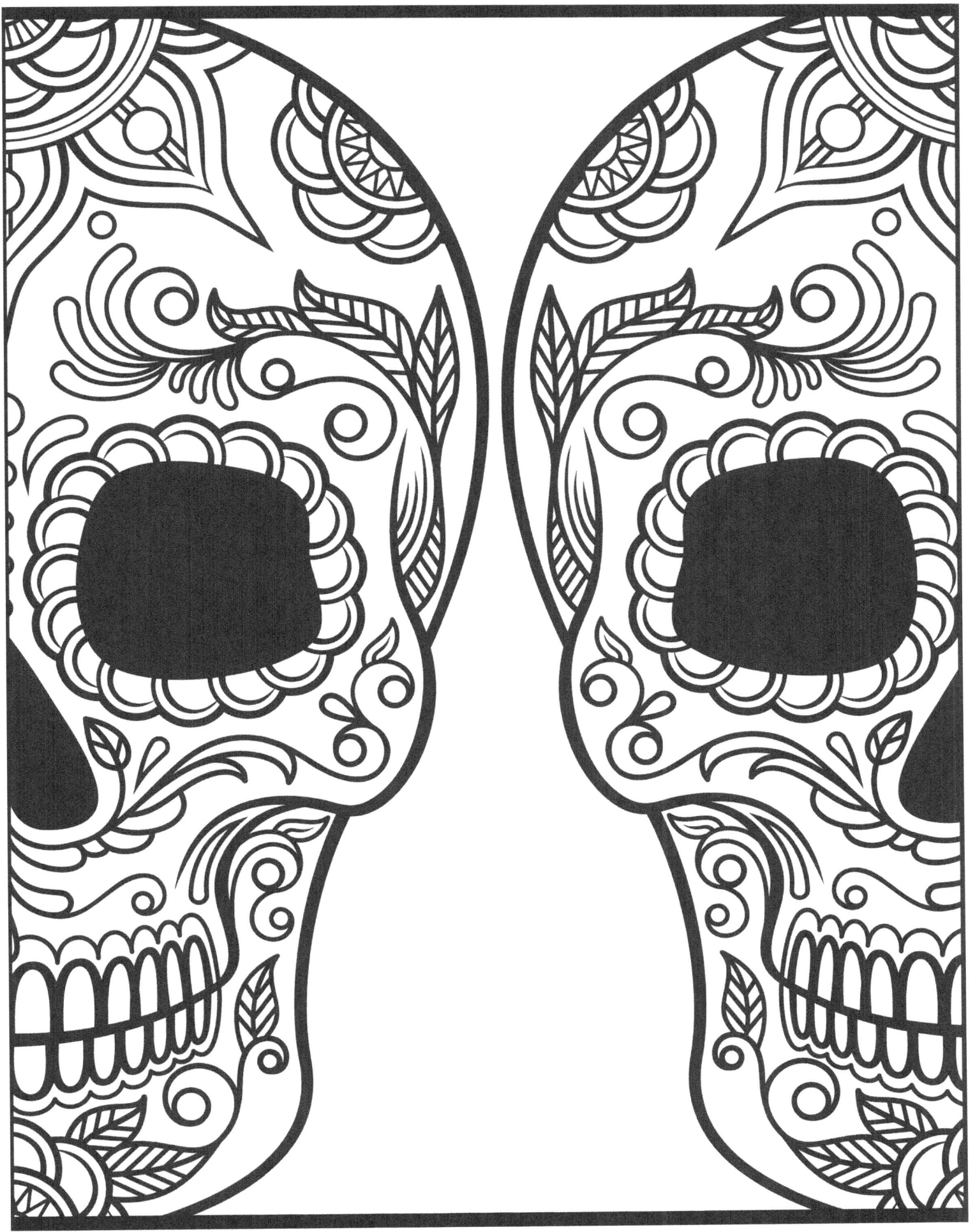

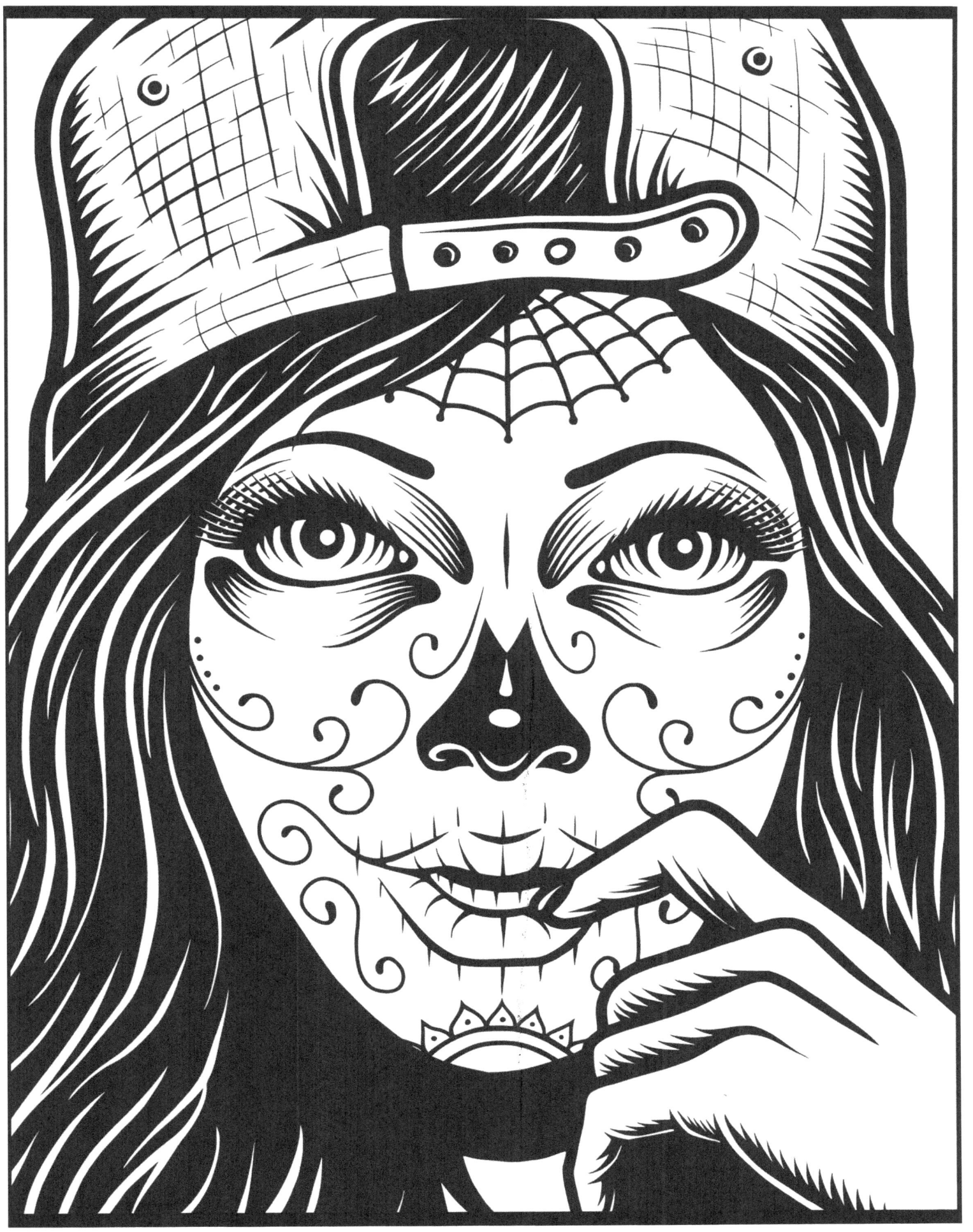

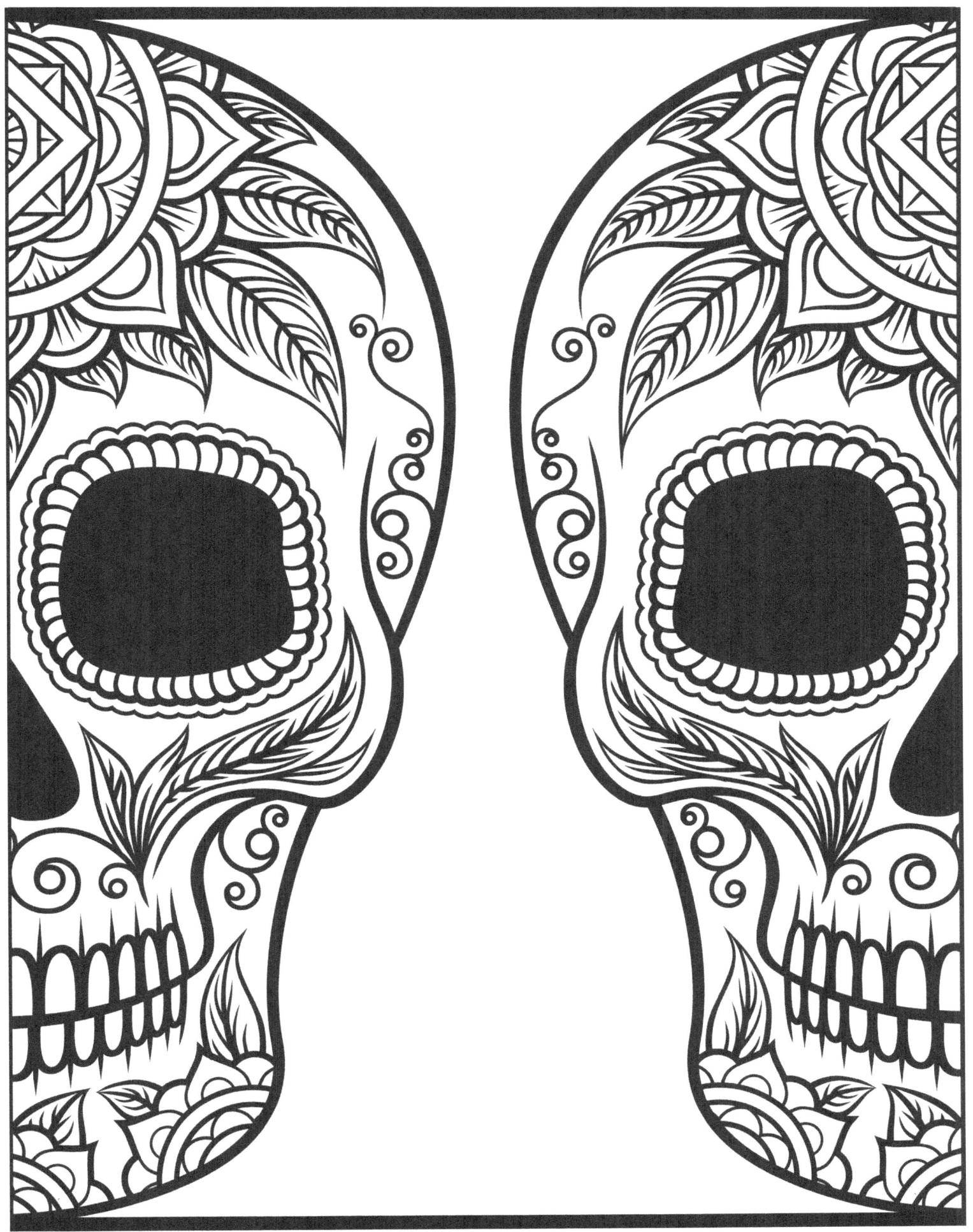

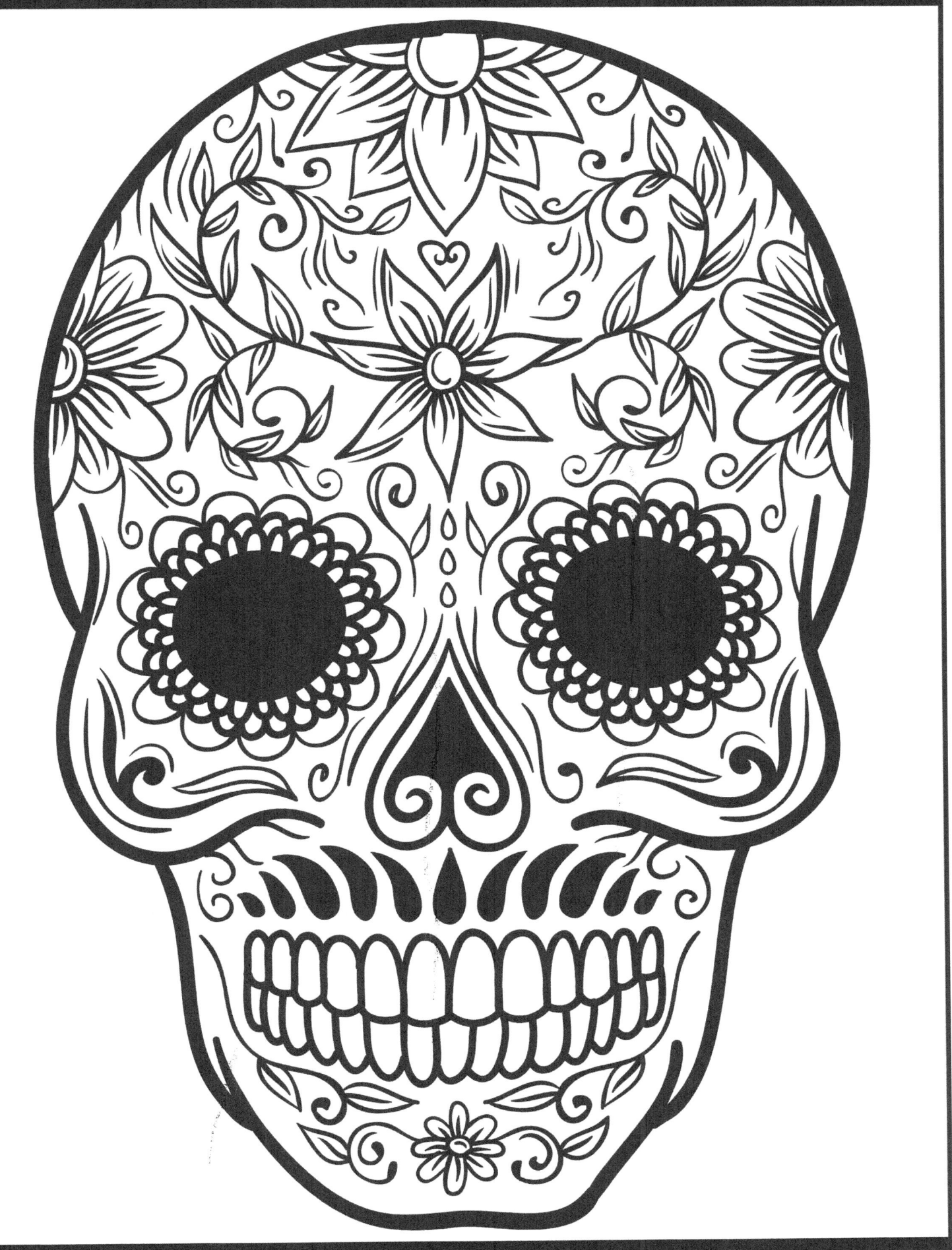

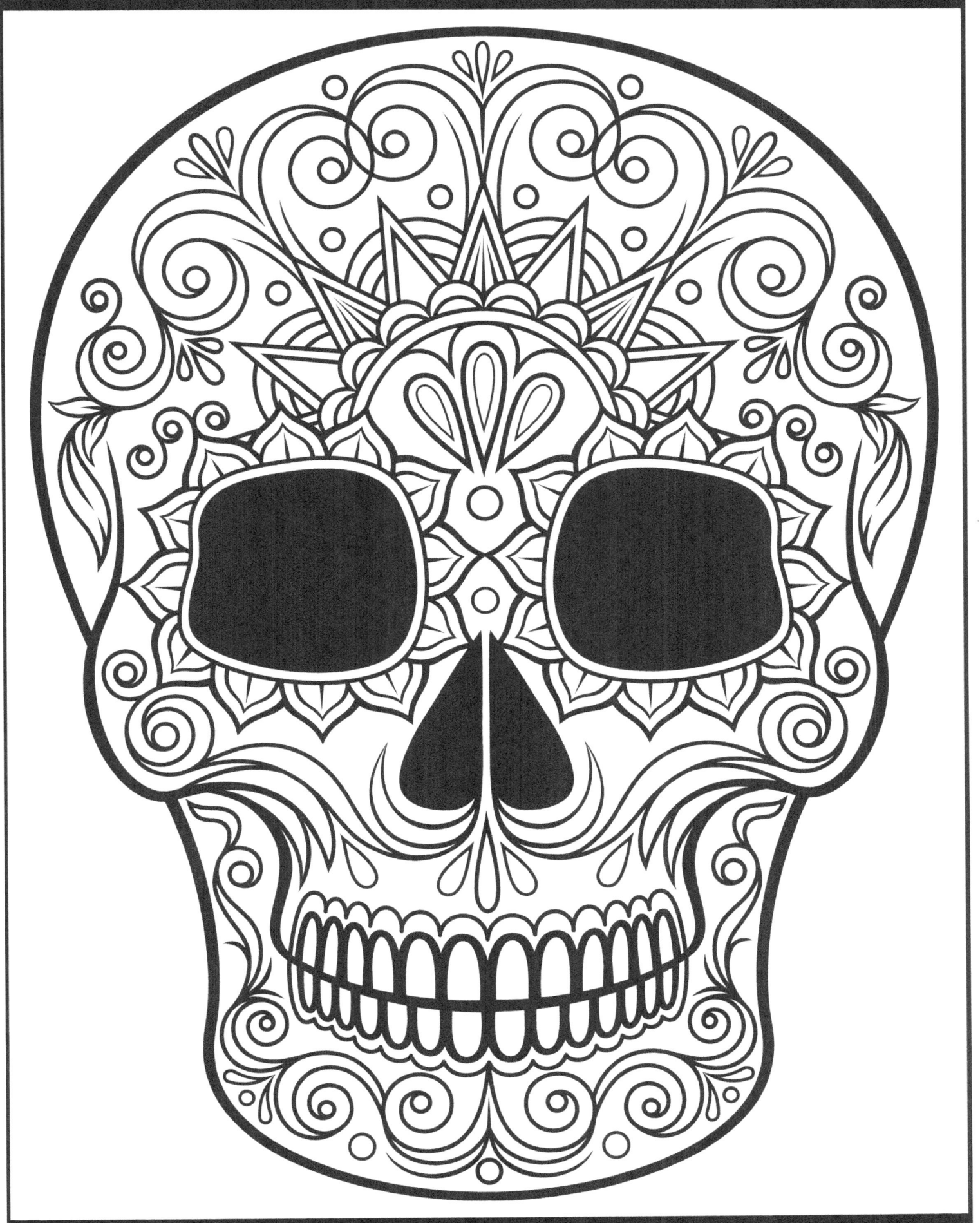

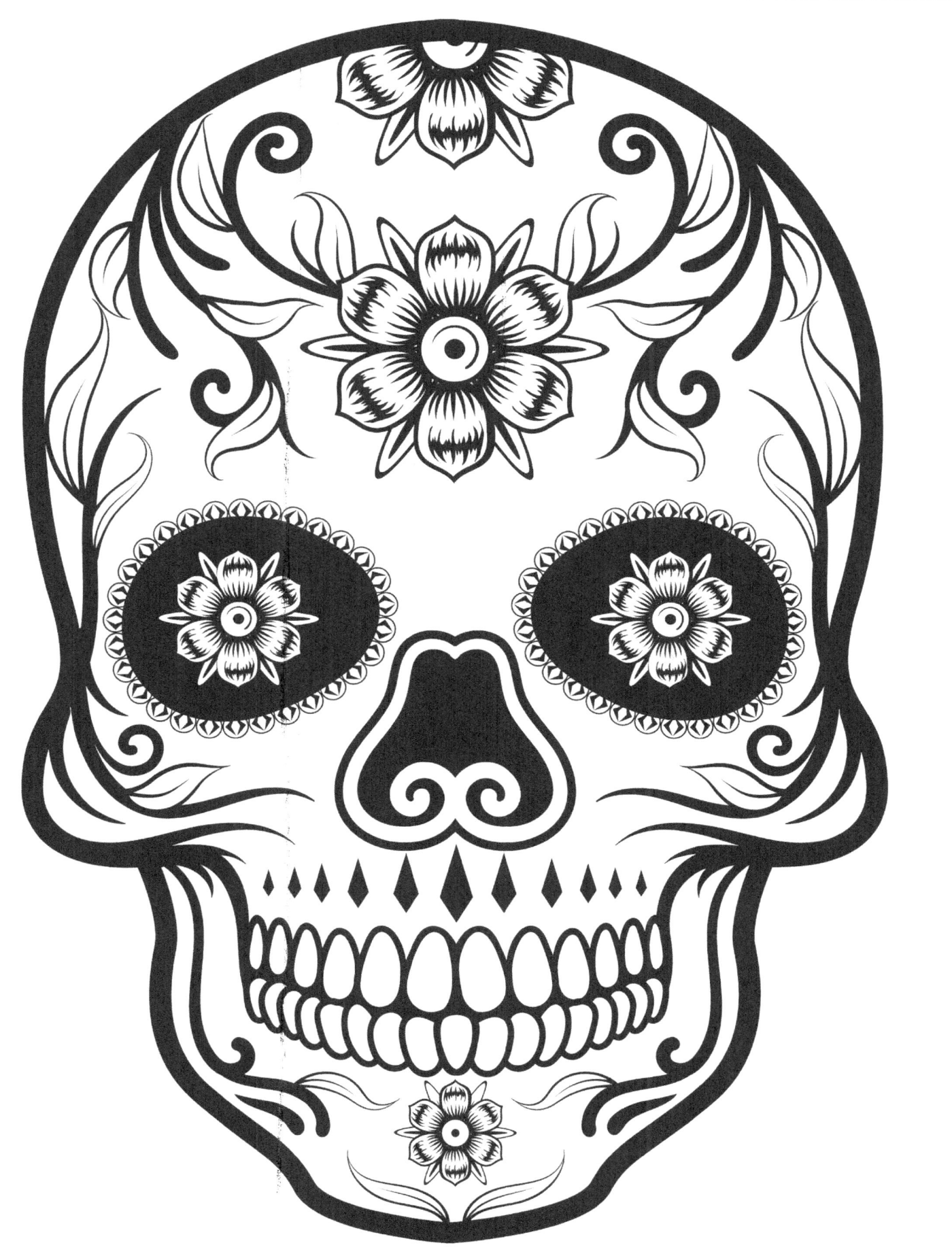

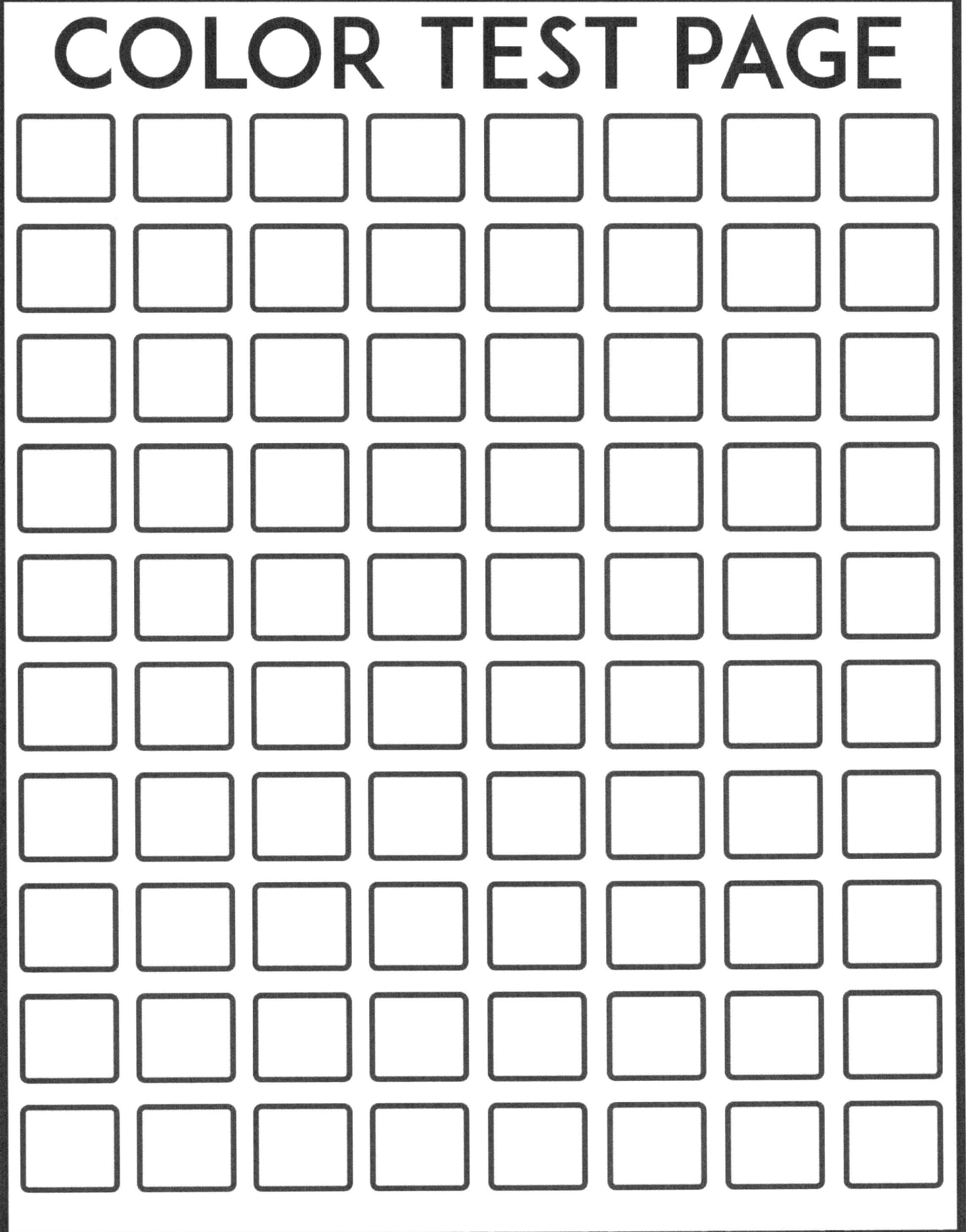

Let's keep in Touch
COME JOIN JABS COMMUNITY

What's that you may ask?

It's my newsletter where you get:

Newletters a month

Updates on my upcoming books and projects

Exclusive contest and giveaways above all

FREE DOWNLOADABLE COLORING PAGES

and more.....

EMAIL US AT
jibransart@gmail.com
TO GET FREE GOODIES!!

JUST TITLE THE EMAIL **"FREEJABS"**
AND WE'LL SEND YOU SOME EXTRA WORKSHEETS
FOR YOU OR YOUR KIDDO TO COLOR ON!!

www.ingramcontent.com/pod-product-compliance
Lightning Source LLC
Chambersburg PA
CBHW080516220526
45465CB00006B/2499